NOT MY OWN

NOT MY OWN

Alfred Martin

MOODY PRESS
CHICAGO

Printed in the United States of America

Contents

CHAPTER   PAGE

1. God's Ownership Through Creation 7

2. Redemption and Stewardship 14

3. The Meaning of Stewardship 21

4. Legal Obligation and Grace Giving 27

5. The First Essential in Giving 35

6. The Extent of His Grace 44

7. Results of His Poverty 57

8. The Christian's Willing Mind 64

9. Money—for Self or for God? 79

10. Stewardship of Body and Mind 91

11. Stewardship of Time, Speech, and Action 99

5

1

God's Ownership Through Creation

In the Bible God says, "Ye are not your own" (1 Cor 6:19). In another passage He asks:

> For who maketh thee to differ from another? And what has thou that thou didst not receive? Now if thou didst receive it, why dost thou glory, as if thou hadst not received it? (1 Cor 4:7).

Our purpose in these pages is to examine the subject of stewardship, which is much broader than many people suppose. The common conception of the subject is that it pertains to what proportion of one's money one may decide to give to God. This approach completely overlooks the true basis of stewardship given in the Bible.

If we really are to understand what stewardship is, we must discover what God tells us about it in His Word. We must begin where He begins and acknowledge that stewardship is, and must be, grounded in the very nature of God and of man. Without this biblical foundation we are left to speculation and may descend to the trivial.

Is stewardship a proper subject for human decision or is it a fundamental fact of man's being? Let us begin at the logical beginning and seek to discover the implications arising from first principles.

GOD THE CREATOR OF ALL THINGS

Men are becoming increasingly aware of the vastness of this universe in which we live. Achievements in orbital flight and space travel have made people conscious of their great environment. Larger and larger telescopes have revealed more and more galaxies studded with multitudes of flaming stars beyond human computation.

What is the result of this expanding knowledge of the universe?

As men make more discoveries about the universe, they are amazed at its immensity. "How great it is!" they rightfully exclaim. But this wonder, this overwhelming sense of awe, which ought to lead to humility, soon is transformed because of the sinfulness of the human heart into self-exalting pride. Because men's minds are blinded by Satan, the "god of this world" (2 Cor 4:4), they are overcome by false conceit. "How great we are," they announce, "because we are finding out so much and because we are making such strides in conquering the vast reaches of space!"

What men ought to say, of course, is, "How great God is, who created all these wonders!"

This universe, whatever men may vainly speculate about it, did not make itself. The Scripture shows that contemplation of the starry heavens and of the earth about us ought to lead to the acknowledgment of God as the Creator. The psalmist sings, "The heavens declare the glory of God; and the firmament sheweth his handiwork" (Psalm 19:1). The apostle Paul explains:

> For the invisible things of him from the creation of the world are clearly seen, being understood by the things that are made, even his eternal power and Godhead; so that they are without excuse (Rom 1:20).

Thoughtful believers frequently have pointed out that no man would be so foolish as to theorize that a watch, for example, or an internal combustion engine could have made itself. The person who examines the inner works of a fine watch recognizes without question that someone made the parts and put them together. He knows without any trouble or doubt that the pistons and valves and other parts of his automobile did not spring into being and into combination by chance.

Yet many of those who freely acknowledge that things around us in everyday life have makers persist in arguing that this marvelous, complicated universe came into being and into its harmonious functioning by some blind chance entirely apart from a Creator. Strangely enough, many of those who theorize in this way are seemingly unaware of any inconsistency on their part.

"In the beginning God created the heaven and the earth" (Gen 1:1). This magnificent opening statement of the Word of God explains the origin of things. True, it does not tell us all that we should like to know, but it does inform us that the answers are found in a Person, the sovereign God.

Other Scripture passages assert the same truth. The New Testament, elaborating on the theme, singles out the Son of God, the Lord Jesus Christ, and attributes creation to Him. "All things were made by him; and without him was not any thing made that was made" (John 1:3).

This creation of all things naturally includes men themselves. We shall examine a little later what the Bible says about this fact and why men ignore or deny it. But whatever men may say, they cannot logically deny that the Scripture makes this claim for God. "God . . . made the world and all things therein" (Acts 17:24). Men are called upon to acknowledge Him who is "the living God, which made heaven, and earth, and the sea, and all things that are therein" (Acts 14:15).

GOD THE OWNER OF ALL THINGS

Since God created all things, it follows that all things belong to Him. It is as simple as that, and this is the basis of all stewardship.

Abraham called God "the most high God, the possessor of heaven and earth" (Gen 14:22). What we call ownership among men is based on many legal considerations, but no matter how well established the human claim may be, all property rights can be traced back ultimately to God. We shall see as we investigate this subject through the Scriptures that God's right of ownership is absolute.

Some passages which help us to see the fact of God's ownership are these:

For all the earth is mine (Exod 19:5).

The earth is the LORD'S, and the fulness thereof; the world, and they that dwell therein. For he hath founded it upon the seas, and established it upon the floods (Psalm 24:1-2).

For every beast of the forest is mine, and the cattle upon a thousand hills. If I were hungry, I would not tell thee: for the world is mine, and the fulness thereof (Psalm 50:10, 12).

The silver is mine, and the gold is mine, saith the LORD of hosts (Hag 2:8).

Thou art worthy, O Lord, to receive glory and honour and power: for thou hast created all things, and for thy pleasure they are and were created (Rev 4:11).

This sampling of passages should be sufficient to show the completeness of God's claim on everything and everybody. *Unless we understand His absolute ownership and see our own relationship to Him, we shall not be in a position to approach the subject of stewardship in any meaningful way.*

Such an approach is entirely different from that of the usual man of the world. He thinks of God, if he thinks of Him at all, as Someone to whom he may give something if he feels like it. God becomes for him a sort of object of charity.

The real question is, does God have the right to do what He wants to do with that which belongs to Him? Can anyone really question this? Many do, but to their own loss and sorrow.

MAN'S UTTER DEPENDENCE ON GOD

It is usual for man to think of himself as self-made and self-sufficient. As a consequence he regards everything he has as his by right. He acts as though he were the owner of his possessions and as though anything he may give to God is given as a favor.

This is a vicious lie, originated by Satan and nurtured by the sinfully inventive mind of man himself.

No man can be self-contained, hence no man has any ground for pride. Basically man has no rights. Just as we must ground our consideration of the subject of stewardship on who and what God is, so we must also found it on who and what man is.

Man, who thinks of himself as self-made, is in reality a creature, that is, a being created by someone else. The psalmist declares, "It is he [that is, God] that hath made us, and not we ourselves" (Psalm 100:3). Everywhere in Scripture God is mentioned as the almighty, sovereign Creator of all things, who gives "to all life, and breath, and all things" (Acts 17:25).

Man, who considers himself self-sufficient, is in reality a dependent being. He could not have brought himself into existence, nor could he last for an instant apart from the sustaining providence of God. While he goes on his way, reckless in his irresponsibility and arrogant in his defiance of his Creator, he is utterly dependent on that Creator for every breath which he draws. "Thou hidest thy face, they are troubled: thou takest away their breath, they die, and return to their dust" (Psalm 104:29). Daniel's accusation against the ungodly Belshazzar was, "The God in whose hand thy breath is, and whose are all thy ways, hast thou not glorified" (Dan 5:23).

Man cannot stop the inevitable process of dying, which has come as God's judgment on sin. The Scripture declares:

> Wherefore, as by one man sin entered into the world, and death by sin; and so death passed upon all men, for that all have sinned (Rom 5:12).

In facing that foe, man is helpless, though at times even in his unbelief he can put up a brave front. Nevertheless, the record is soon written of him, as of all the rest, "And he died" (see, for example, Gen 5:5, 8, 11).

Yes, man is a creature and a dependent being. It follows that *he is a steward, not an owner.* The Bible is filled with reminders that everything we have has come from God. The verses with which this chapter began emphasize this truth. David acknowledged, when the people brought gifts to the Lord in preparation for the future building of the Temple, "All things come of thee, and of thine own have we given thee" (1 Chron 29:14). It is clear that we are nothing of ourselves and have nothing of our own. All that we are and all that we have we received from God; consequently, we and all our possessions belong to Him.

As we have said, it is our purpose in this book to inquire about the meaning of stewardship. This question cannot be settled by human opinion. We shall seek to bring together various passages of the Word of God which speak on the subject.

This study will show us, among other things, that *stewardship is not a mere discussion about money, but is as comprehensive as the whole of life.*

2

Redemption and Stewardship

The Bible tells us that men originally knew of their creation by God and of their responsibility to Him. In their sin, however, they turned away from their Creator.

> Because that, when they knew God, they glorified him not as God, neither were thankful; but became vain in their imaginations, and their foolish heart was darkened (Rom 1:21).

This passage plainly shows us that men are without excuse for their denial or neglect of God (Rom 1:20). Although they could know of His existence and the fact that He is God, if they would but look around and see His handiwork, they prefer to glorify themselves and to enjoy God's creation without acknowledging that it is His.

The picture of mankind painted in the opening chapters of the epistle to the Romans is not a beautiful one; nevertheless it is an accurate one, for God Himself has drawn it. We see man, God's creature, turning to abominable idols, which, because they are nothing, only serve to glorify man himself and to enable him to gratify all his selfish desires in the name of religion.

Idolatry leads to immorality and every kind of foul perversion of God's purpose for mankind. Because of this terrible downward course, man is under the settled "wrath of God" (Rom 1:18). The climax of this divine description of human depravity is horrifying:

> Who knowing the judgment of God, that they which commit such things are worthy of death, not only do the same, but have pleasure in them that do them (Rom 1:32).

What a graphic portrayal of the society about us, in which there is applause for every kind of flagrant sin!

Some may wonder what all this has to do with stewardship. The answer is that man was created to glorify his Maker, but he has fallen from that original state in which God created him and is failing completely in his stewardship. God commanded the first man, Adam, as he stood before his Creator in innocency, to have dominion over the earth in subjection to the will of God (Gen 1:28). Something terrible has happened. Man has disobeyed God and his God-given dominion has been interrupted. We need to see how this came about and what the results are.

The Fall of Man and Stewardship

"God created man in his own image" (Gen 1:27). Man, moreover, was created as a racial being. Adam, the first man, was the head of the race, the ancestor of all men. In His infinite wisdom and love God created human beings as male and female, and ordained marriage while man was still a holy being.

> Therefore shall a man leave his father and his mother, and shall cleave unto his wife: and they shall be one flesh (Gen 2:24).

Into the wonderful environment in which God had placed the man and woman He had made, came the tempter. Genesis 3, the record of the Fall of man, is the explanation of that which follows in the Scripture. Adam and Eve chose to disobey God. In the simple but decisive test which God gave them they utterly failed. They thought of their own desires rather than the command of God. Believing the devil's lie—"Ye shall be like God" (Gen 3:5, literal translation)—they followed the devil's evil suggestion and became not like God but like the devil, rebels against their gracious Creator.

This was the origin of human sin and it affected the whole human race. The New Testament tells us, in a passage to which we previously referred:

> Wherefore, as by one man sin entered into the world, and death by sin; and so death passed upon all men, for that all have sinned (Rom 5:12).

This is only one of many passages in the Bible that show all men to be sinners. Adam became a sinner by sinning. We sin because we are sinners by nature, but the sin is ours and we are responsible for it. We have inherited that evil character which our first parent brought on himself and us (see Eph 2:3).

It is useless for men to rail against this doctrine, to call God unjust, to repudiate God's estimate of them. They cannot escape the judgment of God (Rom 2:3). And when they stop trying to deceive themselves, and look within, they find a gnawing conscience, which the Lord Jesus solemnly warns will be with them forever in hell (Mark 9:46).

God would have been perfectly righteous if He had allowed all men to go into eternal punishment. One of the basic truths we must learn if we are to know about stewardship is that *men have no rights before God.*

But God is rich in mercy.

A New and Added Ground of Stewardship

When man sinned, God could have left him to the unmitigated consequences. God would have had a perfect right to do so; His holiness and righteousness would not have been diminished at all.

But God showed mercy. At the very scene of human rebellion and doom He gave a promise of a coming Redeemer, identified as the seed of the woman (Gen 3:15).

The whole Old Testament is the record of God's merciful dealings with man in preparation for that coming One. The New Testament reveals that God always had a righteous basis for forgiving sin. Peter tells us of this in these words:

> Forasmuch as ye know that ye were not redeemed with corruptible things, as silver and gold, from your vain conversation received by tradition from your fathers; but with the precious blood of Christ, as of a lamb without blemish and without spot: who verily was foreordained before the foundation of the world, but was manifest in these last times for you (1 Pet 1:18-20).

Paul likewise shows that when Christ died He settled the sin question for all those who lived during the time of the Old Testament as well as for those who lived after the cross:

> Being justified freely by his grace through the redemption that is in Christ Jesus: whom God hath set forth to be a propitiation through faith in his blood, to declare his righteousness for the remission of sins that are past, through the forbearance of God; to declare, I say, at this time his righteousness: that he might be just, and the justifier of him which believeth in Jesus (Rom 3:24-26).

These passages show that this is not human opinion,

but God's revealed truth. From all eternity God had His Lamb. The Son of God, the Lord Jesus Christ, came into this world at the appointed time to die for the sins of men.

> For God so loved the world, that he gave his only begotten Son, that whosoever believeth in him should not perish, but have everlasting life (John 3:16).

Man belongs to God by right of creation but is in rebellion against his Maker. Now man has been placed into a new relationship. The death of Christ has put a new and even more pressing claim upon him.

This relationship is expressed by the word *redeemed* in the passage quoted from 1 Peter. This brings to our attention a very important fact in connection with stewardship. We are told that we have been "bought with a price" (1 Cor 6:20).

That price already has been revealed to us. It is far greater than all the silver and gold of this transitory world; it is the "precious blood of Christ" (1 Pet 1:19). Paul, in addressing the Ephesian elders, exhorts them to "feed the church of God, which he hath purchased with his own blood" (Acts 20:28).

Surely this ought to speak plainly to us of the extent and depth of God's love. "God so loved the world, that he gave his only begotten Son" (John 3:16).

The Scripture is explicit in showing that men could not have been saved in any other way. As we have seen, God could have left man alone without providing salvation for him (as He has done, in fact, in the case of the devil and the fallen angels). But if God was to provide salvation at all, He had to do it at infinite cost.

The hymn writer, Cecil F. Alexander, puts it this way in "There Is a Green Hill Far Away":

> There was no other good enough,
> To pay the price of sin;
> He only could unlock the gate
> Of Heav'n and let us in.

No man could redeem any other man, for all were under the same condemnation. The psalmist says:

> None of them can by any means redeem his brother, nor give to God a ransom for him (Psalm 49:7).

Only the sinless, spotless Lamb of God, the Lord Jesus Christ, could bear our sins in His own body on the cross (1 Pet 2:24) and could thereby take away sin by the sacrifice of Himself (Heb 9:26). He "came not to be ministered unto, but to minister, and to give his life a ransom for many" (Mark 10:45).

The Gospel is the most important message that could ever be told by any human being to any other human being. Because the Gospel of Christ offers a perfect salvation, we can understand and fulfill the meaning of stewardship.

DOUBLY HIS

We see then that God has a double claim upon the Christian. Each of us belongs to God because He has created us. Now we realize that we belong to Him also because He has redeemed us.

He says, "Ye are not your own" (1 Cor 6:19).

In many parts of the world over the centuries slavery has been a common social institution. When the New Testament was written slavery was an accepted practice in the Roman Empire.

The slave had no legal rights but belonged entirely to his owner, who had complete control of his person. He had to go where his master commanded and do what his master ordered. He was not his own.

At one time we were the slaves of sin. The Lord Jesus said, "Whosoever committeth sin is the servant [bond-slave] of sin" (John 8:34). Paul reminds us:

> Know ye not, that to whom ye yield yourselves ser-vants to obey, his servants ye are to whom ye obey; whether of sin unto death, or of obedience unto righ-teousness? (Rom 6:16).

Now we have a new Master who has purchased us at infinite cost, having given His own life for us. We be-long to Him completely and absolutely.

THE ESSENCE OF STEWARDSHIP

The most amazing part of this whole subject of stew-ardship is that God, who has this double claim upon us through creation and redemption, does not want any unwilling, sullen slaves who have to serve Him because they have no choice. It is as though He says to the believer in the Lord Jesus Christ, "Yes, you are Mine because I made you; and doubly Mine because I have redeemed you; but I want you to be Mine because you want to be Mine."

Paul was supremely aware of this truth. He knew that God would not force him to surrender his life, but he delighted in calling himself and meaning it from his heart, "Paul, a servant [bondslave] of Jesus Christ" (Rom 1:1).

God therefore is not compelling anyone to be His slave. Rather, He intreats those whom He has saved by His grace to turn their lives over to Him, because He in His infinite wisdom and love is able to do more for them than they could possibly do for themselves.

3

The Meaning of Stewardship

We have seen that man's stewardship is based on God's ownership by right of creation and redemption and that God seeks man's willing acknowledgment of His right. We have not yet inquired about the actual meaning of stewardship.

The words *steward* and *stewardship* do not occur often in the Scriptures, but some of the passages in which they are found help us to understand their meaning.

Paul exhorted the Corinthians:

> Let a man so account of us, as of the ministers of Christ, and stewards of the mysteries of God. Moreover it is required in stewards, that a man be found faithful (1 Cor 4:1-2).

Peter likewise commanded:

> As every man hath received the gift, even so minister the same one to another, as good stewards of the manifold grace of God (1 Pet 4:10).

Paul wrote of his stewardship in these words:

> For if I do this thing willingly, I have a reward: but if against my will, a dispensation [stewardship] of the gospel is committed unto me (1 Cor 9:17).

21

> For this cause I Paul, the prisoner of Jesus Christ for you Gentiles, if ye have heard of the dispensation [stewardship] of the grace of God which is given me to you-ward. . . . That the Gentiles should be fellowheirs, and of the same body, and partakers of his promise in Christ by the gospel (Eph 3:1-2, 6).

> Whereof I am made a minister, according to the dispensation of God [stewardship from God] which is given to me for you, to fulfil the word of God (Col 1:25).

The Greek word from which these words are translated has to do with a household. The noun meaning "stewardship" is the word from which is derived the English word *economy*. A steward is one who manages someone else's household. A stewardship is the management or administration of someone else's household affairs.

These terms are indeed appropriate for the Christian, who is administering property and matters not his own. All the property belongs to God and all the affairs are His. The steward has been appointed by the Owner and is accountable to Him for every detail of his stewardship.

The Lord Jesus Christ gave several parables about stewards, reinforcing the idea expressed in Scripture about the necessity of faithfulness. A steward should have many desirable characteristics. He should be wise and prudent, for he must exercise his judgment in the management of the owner's funds and real estate. Above everything else, however, he must be faithful. This involves honesty, integrity, and complete loyalty to the owner. The steward must lay aside self-interest and think only of the welfare of the one whose property he is administering.

THE DISPENSATIONS

Throughout human history God has given special revelations of Himself to man and has subjected man to various tests and responsibilities on the basis of those revelations. The various periods of testing are known as dispensations. Each dispensation is a particular stewardship, having to do with man's management of God's affairs on this earth.

The dispensational interpretation of Scripture is a literal interpretation and distinguishes different aspects of God's purposes, especially as they pertain to Israel and the Church. In each dispensation man is a steward for God and is accountable to Him.

The present dispensation, usually called the Dispensation of Grace (from Eph 3:2), began with the death of Christ and will continue until He comes again.

COMPLETE SURRENDER

The God who created us and who has redeemed us now beseeches us to present our bodies to Him:

> I beseech you therefore, brethren, by the mercies of God, that ye present your bodies a living sacrifice, holy, acceptable unto God, which is your reasonable service. And be not conformed to this world: but be ye transformed by the renewing of your mind, that ye may prove what is that good, and acceptable, and perfect, will of God (Rom 12:1-2).

The basis on which God makes this appeal is all of that saving work which the Lord Jesus in His grace has accomplished for us. Up to this point everything in the epistle to the Romans has been building up to this plea.

First, men are seen as lost and undone, under the wrath and judgment of God. "There is none righteous, no, not one. For all have sinned, and come short of the glory of God" (Rom 3:10, 23).

Then in the Gospel the righteousness of God has been revealed, being offered as a free gift to all who will believe: "Being justified freely by his grace through the redemption that is in Christ Jesus" (Rom 3:24).

Next the Gospel is seen as giving power for Christian living, so that the believer in Christ is identified with Him in His death and resurrection. This part of the epistle rises to a great climax at the end of chapter 8, where the believer is seen in the purpose of God from eternity past to eternity future, secure and unassailable in His eternal and unchanging love:

> For I am persuaded, that neither death, nor life, nor angels, nor principalities, nor powers, nor things pres-ent, nor things to come, nor height, nor depth, nor any other creature, shall be able to separate us from the love of God, which is in Christ Jesus our Lord (Rom 8:38-39).

Chapters 9 through 11 show the application of the Gospel to God's dispensational purposes for Israel and the Church.

Having pictured for us all these "mercies of God," the apostle beseeches us "brethren" to present our bodies. As believer-priests we have a sacrifice to make, the sacrifice of self. We are not like the Old Testament priests who brought dying sacrifices. We are to live for Him who died for us and rose again (2 Cor 5:14-15).

If stewardship is to have any meaning at all, the be-liever in the Lord Jesus Christ must have come to this point of surrender.

Ideally one should turn over one's life to God at the moment of first accepting Christ. Apparently this is what Paul did when he asked, "Lord, what wilt thou have me to do?" (Acts 9:6). In practice, however, many of us, through ignorance or lack of clear instruction, do not enter in at once to this truth of yieldedness. To us this appeal comes with forcefulness.

A LIVING SACRIFICE

What does it mean for me to present my body as a living sacrifice? It means that I give myself to God unreservedly, that I turn over the control of my life to Him.

Assuredly I ought to do this. I have seen that He has a double claim upon me, the claims of creation and redemption. Yet I do this freely and without compulsion and with full awareness of what I am doing. I do it with great thanksgiving for all He has done for me, and with complete trust that He in His infinite wisdom and love can and will do infinitely more for my good than I could possibly do for myself.

I do it because His love has awakened in me a love in return for Him. "We love him, because he first loved us" (1 John 4:19).

Why have I waited so long to do this? Why did I imagine that I could manage my life better than He? This is the perversity of human nature, to rebel against that which is my "reasonable service."

Now I am His, all that I am and all that I have. I am nothing, of course, and have nothing apart from His grace, but by His grace I have a life to live in service for Him. As Paul said:

> I am crucified with Christ: nevertheless I live; yet not I, but Christ liveth in me: and the life which I now live in the flesh I live by the faith of the Son of God, who loved me, and gave himself for me (Gal 2:20).

Let me not despise, therefore, that little which I am and have. As has often been said, "Little is much when

God is in it." The love of Christ now constrains me; like the apostle, I want to spend and be spent (2 Cor 12:15) in the service of my Lord.

Any property that I have, as well as life itself, is seen in its true perspective as a sacred trust, a divine stewardship. God has put me in trust with some of that which belongs to Him. This truth of the Christian's stewardship of life and property is often referred to in the Scripture. The outstanding qualification of a steward, as we have seen, is given by the Apostle Paul. "It is required in stewards," he reminds us, "that a man be found faithful" (1 Cor 4:2).

4

Legal Obligation and Grace Giving

When the subject of stewardship is mentioned, some people think that the whole of it is comprehended in tithing. If everyone would tithe, they think, this would take care of the matter.

There is nothing wrong with tithing in itself, but the Scripture shows that Christian stewardship is a much broader subject than this and that there is a much higher standard of giving than the tithe.

THE TITHE IN THE OLD TESTAMENT AS AN ACKNOWLEDGMENT

In Old Testament times men acknowledged God's ownership of their lives and property by the payment of a tithe, that is, a tenth, to Him. This, of course, could be wrongly understood. The man who did not realize the significance of it could mistakenly assume that the remaining nine-tenths was his own to do with as he pleased.

The payment of the tithe, however, was an acknowledgment that a man is responsible to God for all the possessions God has given him. In a very real sense God has entrusted him with all these things; that is, He has appointed him a steward.

The earliest mention of the tithe is in the experience of Abraham with Melchizedek, who was king of Salem and priest of the Most High God. Melchizedek appeared suddenly on the scene of history without our being told any of his antecedents, and just as abruptly disappeared from the record. The New Testament explains that God purposely designed the record in this way so that Melchizedek could be a type, or divinely appointed prophetic symbol, of the Lord Jesus Christ, who has an eternal royal priesthood.

Abraham recognized the office of Melchizedek and gave him a tithe of the spoils recovered from those who had captured Sodom and the other cities of the plain. The New Testament exhorts us, "Now consider how great this man was, unto whom even the patriarch Abraham gave the tenth of the spoils" (Heb 7:4). We realize that Abraham paid the tithes to Melchizedek not because of Melchizedek's ownership, but because he was the priest of God Most High, who is the true Owner of man's possessions (Gen 14:22).

We next read of the tithe in the story of Jacob and his dream at Bethel (Gen 28). There he saw a ladder reaching to heaven, with heavenly beings ascending and descending, and heard the voice of God blessing him. He promised God, "Of all that thou shalt give me I will surely give the tenth unto thee" (Gen 28:22). Again we see the tithe as an acknowledgment of God's ownership and His rightful claim on all.

The Tithe and the Law

When God gave the law to Israel through Moses the tithe was included as an integral part of the legal system. The people of Israel were given explicit instructions concerning the tithing of the produce of their fields, their livestock, and their other possessions.

God's command in this regard was:

> And all the tithe of the land, whether of the seed of the land, or of the fruit of the tree, is the LORD'S: it is holy unto the LORD. And if a man will at all redeem ought of his tithes, he shall add thereto the fifth part thereof. And concerning the tithe of the herd, or of the flock, even of whatsoever passeth under the rod, the tenth shall be holy unto the LORD (Lev 27:30-32).

The tithe was not an offering in the strict sense of the term, but an obligation placed on every man under the law. That is, if an Israelite were to keep the law, he did not decide whether he should pay the tithe or not. He had to pay the tithe or become a lawbreaker.

Various kinds of tithes were commanded by the law. The people were to pay tithes to the Levites for their service on behalf of God and the sanctuary.

> And, behold, I have given the children of Levi all the tenth in Israel for an inheritance, for their service which they serve, even the service of the tabernacle of the congregation (Num 18:21).

The Levites in turn were to tithe their tithe.

> Thus speak unto the Levites, and say unto them, When ye take of the children of Israel the tithes which I have given you from them for your inheritance, than ye shall offer up an heave offering of it for the LORD, even a tenth part of the tithe (Num 18:26).

There was also a tithe for the feasts and sacrifices of the Lord, of which the offerer himself and his family partook.

> Thou shalt truly tithe all the increase of thy seed, that the field bringeth forth year by year. And thou shalt eat before the LORD thy God, in the place which he shall choose to place his name there, the tithe of thy corn, of thy wine, and of thine oil, and the firstlings of thy herds

and of thy flocks; that thou mayest learn to fear the LORD thy God always (Deut 14:22-23; see also vv. 24-26).

In addition there was a tithe every third year for the poor (Deut 14:28-29).

Anyone who thinks that the whole of Christian stewardship is tithing has failed to understand the complexity of the legal system and has failed to discriminate between law and grace.

GIVING UNDER THE LAW

It is a common misapprehension to think that the tithe was the complete picture of giving under the law, but even in the Old Testament the tithe was only a part of stewardship. The tithe, it is true, was an obligation on every Israelite, but godly Israelites gave offerings to God in addition to the tithes.

One passage which informs us of this is:

> Then there shall be a place which the LORD your God shall choose to cause his name to dwell there; thither shall ye bring all that I command you; your burnt offerings, and your sacrifices, your tithes, and the heave offering of your hand, and all your choice vows which ye vow unto the LORD (Deut 12:11).

There are indications in the Old Testament that many Israelites disobeyed God and did not bring the tithe as they had been commanded. For this disobedience God brought judgments of various kinds on them.

The prophet Haggai told the people of his day that they were not prospering because they had neglected the building of the Lord's house and its service (see Hag 1:3-11). Malachi brought to the people of his day God's solemn accusation that they had robbed Him:

> Will a man rob God? Yet ye have robbed me. But ye say, Wherein have we robbed thee? In tithes and offer-

ings. Ye are cursed with a curse: for ye have robbed me, even this whole nation. Bring ye all the tithes into the storehouse, that there may be meat in mine house, and prove me now herewith, saith the LORD of hosts, if I will not open you the windows of heaven, and pour you out a blessing, that there shall not be room enough to receive it (Mal 3:8-10).

Many seek to apply these passages directly to the Christian today, but there is no commandment in the New Testament which says that the Christian must tithe. There are, of course, principles of stewardship which can be gleaned from these Old Testament teachings, but—as we shall seek to show—the matter of giving for the believer in Christ in this present Dispensation of Grace is not based on legal obligation.

No one says that the Christian may not tithe if he chooses to do so, but if he holds to the tithe as a legal duty he is misunderstanding the teaching of the Scripture about grace; he would have to *pay* the tithe before he could claim to *give* anything to God.

THE BELIEVER "NOT UNDER THE LAW"

One of the most neglected teachings of Scripture in many parts of the professing Church is the plain statement that the believer in Christ is not under the law.

"For sin shall not have dominion over you," the Apostle Paul assures us, "for ye are not under the law, but under grace" (Rom 6:14). This does not mean that the believer is to be lawless, but it does mean that the Mosaic system has no direct claim upon him.

Many try to separate the law into parts, asserting that one part belongs to the Christian while another part does not. The Scripture always recognizes the law as a unity. "For whosoever shall keep the whole law, and yet offend in one point, he is guilty of all" (James 2:10). The Christian, since he is not under the law, is not under the obligation to tithe.

In rebuttal to this statement, which many would consider radical or unscriptural, some would maintain that tithing is binding upon the Christian because God gave it before the law; it did not orginate with the law. The same could be said for the ordinance of circumcision; God gave this to Abraham before the law. Like tithing, it was incorporated into the law when God gave the law to Israel through Moses. Surely no one, in the light of Acts 15 and the epistle to the Galatians, is going to assert that Christians have to keep the ordinance of circumcision just because it is older than the law.

The trouble often is that when one states what the New Testament teaches—that the believer is not under the law—one is immediately accused, or at least suspected, of being in favor of completely lawless behavior, what the theologians call *antinomianism*, a state of opposition to law or complete lawlessness. Paul shows that the believer is neither under the law, as the Jews were, nor lawless, as the Gentiles were, but in an entirely new relationship, which he speaks of as "under the law to Christ," or "inlawed to Christ" (1 Cor 9:20-21).

The believer has a new position under grace which is neither legalistic nor antinomian. We have been building up to this truth in the preceding studies, as we have noticed God's claims upon us because of creation and redemption. We need now to see how the relationship of grace affects our stewardship.

GRACE LIVING AND GRACE GIVING

To recapitulate some of the things which we have discovered in the Scriptures, we have seen that the believer in the Lord Jesus is in a new relationship to Christ, a position that is neither legalistic nor antinomian. He is not subject to the Mosaic system, nor is he lawless in his conduct, but is personally subject to the Lord Jesus Christ Himself.

Is it wrong then to tithe? Assuredly not, in itself, but on the other hand the New Testament does not command Christians to tithe. If a believer decides in his own heart out of love for the Lord Jesus Christ that he will give a tenth of his earnings to the Lord, he is at liberty to do so and will be blessed in it. But he must not do it as if it were a legal obligation, and he must not do it with the idea that the other nine-tenths are his own to do with as he pleases without consulting the Lord. Many Christians use the tithe as a convenient measuring stick, believing that they ought to be willing under grace to do at least as much as an Israelite was required to do under the law.

If the tithe is not binding, however, upon Christians, does this mean that they are to be careless or random givers? Not if they are to please God. Obligatory tithing, especially if one tries to lay the obligation upon another, is a form of legalism. But random, careless, occasional giving is a form of antinomianism, and we have seen that the believer is not in either of these positions.

What then is to be the standard for a Christian under grace? The Scripture lays down a number of principles for grace giving. In subsequent chapters we shall examine these principles as they relate to the giving of money as well as to other aspects of life.

Just as the believer has been saved by God's grace, so he is to live by God's grace. His stewardship of money is to be in the sphere of grace. He will find as he studies what the Word of God tells him about the use of money,

and as he obeys its teachings, that he will have unprec-
edented and indescribable joy in giving.

Once we realize that God has taken the whole matter
out of the sphere of legal obligation and placed it in the
sphere of grace, it takes on an entirely different aspect.

5

The First Essential in Giving

Any study of Christian stewardship must draw heavily on the teaching of the central passage in the New Testament on the subject. That passage is found in 2 Corinthians 8 and 9. We need now to consider this important passage and to examine several corollary passages in other parts of the New Testament.

A great project of Paul's third missionary journey was the collection for the saints at Jerusalem (see 1 Cor 16:1). In writing to the Corinthians about the part they were to have in this collection, Paul used the example of the churches of Macedonia to encourage and motivate the Corinthian believers.

The giving of the Macedonian Christians was a result, we are told, of the grace of God (2 Cor 8:1). Although they were poor in material things, they excelled in generosity and liberality (v. 2). They were like the poor widow noted by the Lord Jesus, who gave more than all the rest who cast money into the treasury of the Lord, even though her offering was only two mites, the smallest possible coins. Her gift was more than the others because she gave all she had (Mark 12:41-44). Those who talk glibly about giving the widow's mite, when they contribute only a pittance out of a comfortable supply, do not know what they are talking about, or, worse still, are dishonoring God.

Many preachers of our day would faint dead away in the pulpit if the congregation begged them to accept more of an offering than they could reasonably be expected to give. Yet such was the attitude of the Macedonian Christians in Paul's day.

Some church leaders today use unscriptural and unseemly methods in pressuring people to give money to the Lord's work; as a reaction against that, some sincere, godly ministers hesitate even to mention money from the pulpit. Yet the Bible says much about money and its place in the Lord's service.

If Christians can learn what the Bible says about this important subject, they will not have to be cajoled, threatened, browbeaten, or pressured into giving to the Lord. The Macedonians gave joyfully of their means because they had learned the first essential of Christian stewardship.

What Is the First Essential?

This first essential in Christian giving and in all Christian stewardship, as the Macedonian Christians had learned, is the giving of self to the Lord. If one gives oneself to God, then it follows that everything one has belongs to God. But if one has not taken this first step, then naturally the next step will not be possible. As long as even a believer considers his life his own there can be no real Christian stewardship.

We often say that we have dedicated our lives to God, but belie it by our actions. The pocketbook is a sort of acid test of the reality of our surrender. The Macedonians gave far beyond the expectation of the apostle toward the offering for the saints because they had first given themselves to the Lord.

And this they did, not as we hoped, but first gave their

own selves to the Lord, and unto us by the will of God (2 Cor 8:5).

In exhorting the Corinthians to follow this example, Paul reminded them of their superiority in other lines of Christian activity. In spite of their many failures and shortcomings, many of them did abound in faith and in the other virtues mentioned (v. 7). Paul longed to see them excel "in this grace also." He identifies giving to the Lord as a grace; it becomes a reflection of what God has done for us. We are the recipients of His grace, and He creates within us a desire to be gracious also.

One should note that the apostle expressly says that he is not commanding the Christians to give (v. 8). He would encourage them to emulate others who have done so much, and he suggests this as a way to prove the sincerity of their love. They say that they love the Lord Jesus Christ and their fellowmen. Let them show this in reality.

James has something to say about a mere profession of faith that is not genuine:

> If a brother or sister be naked, and destitute of daily food, and one of you say unto them; Depart in peace, be ye warmed and filled; notwithstanding ye give them not those things which are needful to the body; what doth it profit? Even so faith, if it hath not works, is dead, being alone (James 2:15-17).

The Scripture does not hesitate to say that the Christian's use of money is a test of the reality of his profession and of his love for the Lord Jesus.

CHRIST THE SUPREME EXAMPLE OF GIVING

In this central passage in the Bible on the subject of Christian stewardship the Lord Jesus Christ is presented as the supreme Example of giving.

> For ye know the grace of our Lord Jesus Christ, that,
> though he was rich, yet for your sakes he became poor,
> that ye through his poverty might be rich (2 Cor 8:9).

Grace is God's favor shown toward those who deserve
only His condemnation. It cannot be deserved or mer-
ited. It cannot be earned in any way. It can never be paid
for. In Romans Paul clearly shows that grace and works
are mutually exclusive:

> And if by grace, then it is no more of works: otherwise
> grace is no more grace. But if it be of works, then is it no
> more grace: otherwise work is no more work (Rom 11:6).

Grace is freely bestowed by the sovereign God.

The "grace of our Lord Jesus Christ" is seen, we are
told, in the fact that "though he was rich, yet for your
sakes he became poor, that ye through his poverty might
be rich." In view of the assertion that He was rich, we
might well inquire how rich He was; this will aid us in
discovering something of the extent of His grace.

How rich was the Lord Jesus? This is a question that is
almost unanswerable. To ask how rich the Lord Jesus
was is to ask in effect how rich God is, because the Lord
Jesus Christ is God. The Scripture declares His deity
without equivocation and without qualification. He is
one of the Persons of the eternal Godhead. Some of the
passages which tell this are these:

> In the beginning was the Word, and the Word was
> with God, and the Word was God (John 1:1).

> And we know that the Son of God is come, and hath
> given us an understanding, that we may know him that
> is true, and we are in him that is true, even in his Son
> Jesus Christ. This is the true God, and eternal life (1 John
> 5:20).

> Who hath delivered us from the power of darkness,

and hath translated us into the kingdom of his dear Son.
. . . Who is the image of the invisible God, the firstborn of
every creature: for by him were all things created, that
are in heaven, and that are in earth, visible and invisible,
whether they be thrones, or dominions, or prin-
cipalities, or powers: all things were created by him, and
for him: and he is before all things, and by him all things
consist (Col 1:13, 15-17).

Whose are the fathers, and of whom as concerning the
flesh Christ came, who is over all, God blessed for ever.
Amen (Rom 9:5).

We have seen that God is the Creator and Possessor of
all things. The universe came into being at His word.
Consequently all this vast creation belongs to the Lord
Jesus Christ, the Son of God. "All things were made by
him; and without him was not any thing made that was
made" (John 1:3).

For by him were all things created, that are in heaven,
and that are in earth . . . all things were created by him,
and for him (Col 1:16).

God . . . hath in these last days spoken unto us by his
Son, whom he hath appointed heir of all things, by
whom also he made the worlds; who being the bright-
ness of his glory, and the express image of his person,
and upholding all things by the word of his power, when
he had by himself purged our sins, sat down on the right
hand of the Majesty on high (Heb 1:1-3).

Since Jesus Christ is God, all that exists owes its existence to Him, belongs to Him, and is under His control.

If we think then of the riches of the Lord Jesus Christ,
this is the first thing that occurs to us. He was rich in
being the Possessor of heaven and earth. But He was also
rich in other ways.

God created not only the material universe that can be

seen, but also an invisible creation, which is without doubt far greater than that which we can see. We read in the Scripture of multitudes of holy heavenly beings who perform the service of God. These are ordinarily referred to as the angels. Here and there in the Scripture the curtain is drawn aside, as it were, and God permits us to have a glimpse of that which is otherwise invisible and unknown to us.

One such example is seen in the experience of Elisha and the young man at Dothan:

> And when the servant of the man of God was risen early, and gone forth, behold, an host compassed the city both with horses and chariots. And his servant said unto him, Alas, my master! How shall we do? And he answered, Fear not: for they that be with us are more than they that be with them. And Elisha prayed, and said, Lord, I pray thee, open his eyes, that he may see. And the Lord opened the eyes of the young man; and he saw: and, behold, the mountain was full of horses and chariots of fire round about Elisha (2 Kings 6:15-17).

One familiar passage speaks of an "innumerable company of angels" (Heb 12:22). John saw a multitude of angels around the throne of God which he describes as "ten thousand times ten thousand, and thousands of thousands" (Rev 5:11). These are spirit beings, messengers and servants of God, completely devoted to their Creator and perfectly subject to His will. The writer to the Hebrews, quoting from Psalm 104:4 and Psalm 45:6, says:

> And of the angels he saith, Who maketh his angels spirits, and his ministers a flame of fire. But unto the Son he saith, Thy throne, O God, is for ever and ever: a sceptre of righteousness is the sceptre of thy kingdom (Heb 1:7-8).

The passage concludes, concerning the angels:

> Are they not all ministering spirits, sent forth to minister for them who shall be heirs of salvation? (Heb 1:14).

From the time they were created, the heavenly beings have worshiped and praised their sovereign God. Isaiah had a vision of the throne of God in which he saw the seraphim (the word, occurring only here, apparently means "burning ones"), holy heavenly beings of a high order, around God's throne, ardent in their devotion, and calling out to one another:

> Holy, holy, holy, is the LORD of hosts: the whole earth is full of his glory (Isa 6:3).

John quotes from this passage in Isaiah and comments:

> These things said Esaias [Isaiah], when he saw his [Christ's] glory, and spake of him (John 12:41).

The passage is clear; it cannot be construed in any other way. It was the glory of the Lord Jesus that Isaiah saw when he saw the glory of God. It was the Lord Jesus whom the seraphim were worshiping.

On the night before His death, looking toward the accomplishment of His work upon the cross, the Lord Jesus prayed:

> And now, O Father, glorify thou me with thine own self with the glory which I had with thee before the world was (John 17:5).

From the time they were created, the heavenly beings did not cease to worship, adore, and praise the Son of God. He was the recipient of honor and glory.

It is hard for us to realize the wonders and glories of heaven, where the Lord Jesus Christ was rightfully the center of attention of all the marvelous intelligences He had created. We are given only brief and partial glimpses in the Scripture, but we can see enough to realize that "he was rich."

THE ACME OF HIS RICHES

We have considered some ways in which the Lord Jesus Christ was rich, but what we have mentioned thus far does not begin to describe His riches alluded to in the text on which we are meditating. It is true that He is the Owner of all things, the whole universe, by right of creation, and the object of worship of all the holy angels. Nevertheless His riches were vastly greater than that.

The acme of His riches consisted in the fact that as one of the Persons of the eternal Godhead He was the object of infinite love and enjoyed the bliss of infinite fellowship from all eternity. We cannot even begin to imagine the depths of perfect harmony among the Persons of the Godhead—the Father, the Son, and the Holy Spirit—as They have always existed in all Their infinite perfection. God is one God, but He exists in three Persons, and each of these Persons is both the subject and the object of infinite love. We see something of this love as it is expressed in the Scriptures. The Lord Jesus said to the Father:

> Father, I will that they also, whom thou hast given me, be with me where I am; that they may behold my glory, which thou hast given me: for thou lovedst me before the foundation of the world (John 17:24).

The Scripture declares, "The Father loveth the Son, and hath given all things into his hand" (John 3:35); and again, "For the Father loveth the Son, and sheweth him all things that himself doeth" (John 5:20).

At the baptism of the Lord Jesus the voice of the Father

was heard from heaven saying, "This is my beloved Son, in whom I am well pleased" (Matt 3:17). As He said this to John the Baptist and others, He said directly to the Lord Jesus, "Thou art my beloved Son, in whom I am well pleased" (Mark 1:11).

Later, on the mount of transfiguration, he said again, "This is my beloved Son, in whom I am well pleased; hear ye him" (Matt 17:5). The Father made clear His supreme and infinite love for His Son.

Because God is the only perfect and infinite Being, His greatest love must necessarily and rightly be for Himself. This is not a selfish love, but a righteous love, a mutual love shared among the three Persons of the Godhead. Each of the Persons, as we have seen, is both the subject and the object of perfect love, as well as being aware of each of the other Persons as the subject and the object of perfect love. This is almost incomprehensible to us but may enable us to see dimly how rich the Lord Jesus Christ really was.

Unless we have some recognition of His riches we shall not be able to understand at all the extent of His grace in becoming poor for our sakes.

6

The Extent of His Grace

The grace of our Lord Jesus Christ consists in the fact that though He was rich He became poor for our sakes. We have sought to see how rich He was. We have now to inquire how poor He became. When we pursue this inquiry we are confronted with this great truth that the eternal Son of God became a man. A parallel passage to the text we are considering (2 Cor 8:9) is found in these words:

> Let this mind be in you, which was also in Christ Jesus: who, being in the form of God, thought it not robbery to be equal with God: but made himself of no reputation, and took upon him the form of a servant, and was made in the likeness of men: and being found in fashion as a man, he humbled himself, and became obedient unto death, even the death of the cross (Phil 2:5-8).

The truth of the Person of Christ is one of the greatest mysteries of the Christian faith. We cannot understand how the same Person can have two natures—can be both God and man—yet we know that this is so because the Word of God teaches it. The Son of God, in becoming a human being, assumed all the sinless limitations of humanity, even though He retained all His undiminished deity.

The statement that He existed in the form of God is an indication of His eternal deity. The word *form* does not

44

refer to mere outward appearance but to the manifestation of essential inner being. There has often been controversy about just what the Lord Jesus laid aside in becoming man. The theory of some, that He gave up His deity, is impossible. God cannot stop being God, for an essential quality of His being is His eternity and immutability. The Lord Jesus Christ always has been God and always will be God. Nor could He give up the attributes or characteristics of God, for the attributes make up the nature. God, in the very nature of things, could not allow the diminution or cessation of any facet of His being.

That these things are so is witnessed by the scenes which we have of the earthly life and ministry of the Lord Jesus in the gospels. There we see Him manifesting His deity on various occasions.

What did He lay aside? He emptied Himself of all self-interest. He laid aside the glory and honor that were rightfully His as one of the Persons of the Godhead. This is the meaning of that rather puzzling clause, that He "thought it not robbery to be equal with God." He did not consider this being on an equality with God a thing to be seized or held onto.

OUR LORD'S SELF-HUMBLING

Some might wonder perhaps why we are giving so much attention in a study of stewardship to the doctrinal truths of Christ's incarnation and death for us. The answer is found, of course, in the usual Scripture practice of mingling doctrine with practical truth for Christian living. Our stewardship is a result of His stewardship. The Lord Jesus Christ is the supreme Example in this regard.

Just as the Lord Jesus always existed in the *form* of God, so He took upon Himself the *form* of a servant (Phil

2:7). Again we see it is not mere appearance. He did not merely seem like a servant or act like a servant; He became a servant in the truest sense. Furthermore, the word translated "servant" means literally a "bond-slave." We see an illustration of this in His washing of His disciples' feet on the night before His death (John 13:4-5). This was the constant attitude of our Lord, who said:

> For even the Son of man came not to be ministered unto, but to minister, and to give his life a ransom for many (Mark 10:45).

It would seem that the assumption of human nature would in itself be sufficient humbling for the Son of God, but we read further that "being found in fashion as a man, he humbled himself, and became obedient unto death, even the death of the cross" (Phil 2:8).

The significance of His death will be dealt with a little later in our study. At this point, however, it would be well for us to note that the Lord Jesus went voluntarily to the cross for us. This was His purpose in coming into the world, as many passages of Scripture teach. He did this for us; that is, His death was vicarious, or substitutionary. "For your sakes he became poor" (2 Cor 8:9).

And such a death—the death of the cross! Not a noble, honorable death in the eyes of the world, for the Roman law reserved crucifixion for the lowest type of criminals who did not have the privilege of Roman citizenship. This was the death which He endured for you and for me. But it was a victorious death. On the cross He exclaimed, "It is finished" (John 19:30). He accomplished that which He had come into the world to do.

How Poor Did He Become?

Just as we have examined the riches of the Lord Jesus

under various aspects, so now we can see different ways in which He became poor for us. All of this will help us to understand better the extent of His grace.

We read in the Scripture that the Lord Jesus came into the world in the midst of physical and material poverty. Mary, His mother, and her husband Joseph, although they came from the royal line of David, were poor people. When the Lord Jesus was born in Bethlehem He was wrapped in swaddling clothes and placed in a manger "because there was no room for them in the inn" (Luke 2:7). Probably room could have been found, in spite of the terribly crowded conditions brought about by the enrollment, if Joseph and Mary had been wealthy.

An even clearer indication of their poverty, however, is seen in the account of the presentation of the infant Jesus in the Temple at the age of forty days. His mother offered "a pair of turtledoves, or two young pigeons," and this was said to be a "sacrifice according to that which is said in the law of the Lord" (Luke 2:24). The usual offering designated in the law of the Lord was "a lamb of the first year for a burnt offering, and a young pigeon, or a turtledove, for a sin offering" (Lev 12:6). But the offering which Mary brought was that designated in the law of Moses for the mother who could not afford a lamb:

> And if she be not able to bring a lamb, then she shall bring two turtles [turtledoves], or two young pigeons; the one for the burnt offering, and the other for a sin offering (Lev 12:8).

As He grew to manhood the Lord Jesus had no earthly possessions of His own. We see the amazing paradox of the Creator and Possessor of heaven and earth walking about in this world with nothing. When He was asked about paying tribute to Caesar He asked someone else to

produce a coin for Him to exhibit to enforce His teaching
(Matt 22:19). He said to a man who promised to follow
Him:

> The foxes have holes, and the birds of the air have
> nests; but the Son of man hath not where to lay his head
> (Matt 8:20; see also Luke 9:58).

Homeless, and almost friendless, He walked along the
dusty roads of Galilee and Judea, dependent—humanly
speaking—on the material support provided by faithful
ones such as the godly women from Galilee whom Luke
mentions:

> And it came to pass afterward, that he went through-
> out every city and village, preaching and shewing the
> glad tidings of the kingdom of God: and the twelve were
> with him, and certain women, which had been healed of
> evil spirits and infirmities, Mary called Magdalene, out
> of whom went seven devils, and Joanna the wife of
> Chuza Herod's steward, and Susanna, and many others,
> which ministered unto him of their substance (Luke
> 8:1-3).

The Lord Jesus owned no real estate and left no possessions. When He was upon the cross He evidently had
nothing except the clothes He had worn. The soldiers
who cruficied Him divided these, gambling for His
seamless outer garment (see Matt 27:35; Mark 15:24;
Luke 23:34; John 19:23-24).

Not in the midst of worldly prestige, power, or wealth
did the Son of God come. His poverty was evident for all
to see. No one could accuse Him of taking from the poor
to enrich Himself. No, He became the poorest of the poor
for our sakes.

Yet the physical and material poverty which the Lord
Jesus assumed was only a minor part of the poverty
referred to in the text. Many people have lived in pov-

erty and in that condition have accomplished much and served their generation well. The Scripture does not place any undue emphasis on the fact that the Lord Jesus was poor in this sense, although it does draw to our attention the astounding contrast of His previous glory and His earthly condition.

But not only did the Creator of heaven and earth come into this world with nothing; also the object of worship of the angelic hosts came into this world to endure the neglect and denial, and even the taunts and sneers, of men. Isaiah prophesied of Him:

> He is despised and rejected of men; a man of sorrows, and acquainted with grief: and we hid as it were our faces from him; he was despised, and we esteemed him not (Isa 53:3).

One can recall some of the horrible and untrue and blasphemous charges made against the Lord of glory by evil-minded sinners:

> Say we not well that thou art a Samaritan, and hast a devil? (John 8:48).

> Behold a gluttonous man, and a winebibber, a friend of publicans and sinners! (Luke 7:34).

> He hath Beelzebub, and by the prince of the devils casteth he out devils (Mark 3:22).

Well might the writer to the Hebrews exhort us:

> For consider him that endured such contradiction of sinners against himself, lest ye be wearied and faint in your minds (Heb 12:3).

No one ever was more misunderstood than the Lord Jesus.

> He was in the world, and the world was made by him, and the world knew him not. He came unto his own

[things], and his own [people] received him not (John
1:10-11).

Even some members of His own family, half brothers
according to the flesh, taunted Him about His ministry
because they did not believe in Him (John 7:3-5). Even
some of His friends "went out to lay hold on him: for
they said, He is beside himself" (Mark 3:21).

As His ministry progressed, the intensity of opposition increased. The Gospel of John shows very dramati-
cally this progressively more serious conflict between
light and darkness, between love and hate, between life
and death.

HEAVENLY PRAISE AND EARTHLY HOWLS

The religious leaders and their followers became increasingly hostile and increasingly bitter against the
Lord Jesus and progressively more cruel in their treat-
ment of Him. On several occasions they took up stones
to stone Him, but were unable to do so, "because his
hour was not yet come" (John 7:30; 8:20).

Eventually, though, the hour did come, that foreor-
dained hour for which He had come into the world. As
the mob with their frenzied leaders stood before Pilate
and he offered to release the Lord Jesus, they roared,
"Not this man, but Barabbas" (John 18:40). Peter later
described that event in these words:

> The God of Abraham, and of Isaac, and of Jacob, the
> God of our fathers, hath glorified his Son Jesus; whom ye
> delivered up, and denied him in the presence of Pilate,
> when he was determined to let him go. But ye denied the
> Holy One and the Just, and desired a murderer to be
> granted unto you; and killed the Prince of life, whom
> God hath raised from the dead; whereof we are witnesses
> (Acts 3:13-15).

In response to Pilate's question, "What shall I do then with Jesus which is called Christ?" they yelled back their bloodthirsty answer, "Let him be crucified" (Matt 27:22-23). "Crucify him," they shouted (Mark 15:13-14).

He was beaten, He was spit upon, He was tormented; a crown of thorns was pressed into His brow; He was nailed hand and foot to a cross. And there before the gaze of all—with the disciples, for the most part, standing far off—He still endured the "contradiction of sinners against himself" (Heb 12:3). One can see the hateful priests and other religious leaders wagging their heads at Him in gleeful malice, as they cried:

> He saved others; himself he cannot save. If he be the King of Israel, let him now come down from the cross, and we will believe him (Matt 27:42).

> He trusted on the LORD that he would deliver him: let him deliver him, seeing he delighted in him (Psalm 22:8).

This is a part of the poverty of the Lord Jesus. We hear it in the contrasting sounds of the heavenly chorus and the earthly mob:

"Holy, holy holy, is the LORD of hosts," joyously and reverently exclaimed the seraphim as they beheld His glory (Isa 6:3; cf John 12:41). "Glory to God in the highest," proclaimed the heavenly host on the night of Christ's birth (Luke 2:14).

"Crucify him, crucify him," demanded the sinful human throng.

What a difference was experienced by the Son of God, who had been rich and who became poor for our sakes!

THE DEPTH OF HIS POVERTY

What was the true depth of the poverty of the Lord Jesus? It was not that He had no earthly possessions,

although this was true. It was not that He endured the
hatred and persecution of men, although that was true
also. The Scripture says little about the material poverty
of the Lord Jesus, and lays slight stress upon the details
of His physical suffering.

Far greater than what the Lord Jesus suffered at the
hands of sinful men was what He suffered at the hand of
His heavenly Father. This is expressed in the words of
prophecy:

> All we like sheep have gone astray; we have turned
> every one to his own way; and the Lord hath laid on him
> the iniquity of us all (Isa 53:6).

And again, in the same marvelous passage:

> Yet it pleased the Lord to bruise him; he hath put him
> to grief: when thou shalt make his soul an offering for
> sin, he shall see his seed, he shall prolong his days, and
> the pleasure of the Lord shall prosper in his hand (Isa
> 53:10).

The New Testament reinforces this in these words:

> Him who knew no sin he made to be sin on our behalf;
> that we might become the righteousness of God in him (2
> Cor 5:21, ASV).

When our Lord prayed in the Garden of Gethsemane
the night before He went to the cross, He said, "O my
Father, if it be possible, let this cup pass from me" (Matt
26:39). Many have been perplexed about the meaning of
these words. Some have even supposed that the Lord
Jesus Christ was afraid to die. This is unthinkable. Many
brave men have faced death without flinching; could it
be said of the Lord of glory that He was any less coura-
geous?

What was this cup? Surely it was not death as such.
Surely it was not merely the agony of physical suffering.

Assuredly it was an experience which no one else could face. The Lord Jesus, who never had had any personal experience of sin, was facing the prospect of being made sin. God was to judge Him for all the sin of the world, just as if it were His own. What must it have meant to a personally sinless Person to be made sin? We cannot begin to imagine the agony of His holy soul.

But the Lord Jesus Christ did not stop with the plea, "Let this cup pass from me." In fact, He prefaced the prayer with the conditional clause, "If it be possible." Then He went on immediately to say, "Nevertheless not my will, but thine, be done" (Luke 22:42; cf. Matt 26:39; Mark 14:36). When, later, His enemies came to take Him, He asked, "The cup which my Father hath given me, shall I not drink it?" (John 18:11).

With perfect and complete surrender to the Father's will (not a rebellious, grudging, regretful surrender, but a joyous, willing surrender), the Lord Jesus Christ our Saviour went resolutely to the cross, drinking to the dregs the cup of judgment from the hand of the righteous Judge.

How poor did the Lord Jesus Christ become for our sakes? If we really want to know the depth of His poverty, then we must stand in faith at the foot of the cross on which He died and there in that thick darkness we must listen to the agonizing cry, "My God, my God, why hast thou forsaken me?" (Matt 27:46).

What does this mean? Did God really forsake His Son as He hung upon the cross? Not in every sense of the term, for Christ Himself is God, and we also read that "God was in Christ, reconciling the world unto himself, not imputing their trespasses unto them" (2 Cor 5:19).

Yet there is a very true and deep sense in which God did forsake the Lord Jesus on the cross. What other meaning could be attached to the poignant question?

God the righteous Judge was judging the sin of mankind. Earlier John the Baptist had pointed to Christ, saying, "Behold the Lamb of God, which taketh away the sin of the world" (John 1:29).

Quoting from the prophecy in Isaiah 53, the Apostle Peter speaks of Christ's death in these words:

> Who his own self bare our sins in his own body on the tree, that we, being dead to sins, should live unto righteousness: by whose stripes ye were healed (1 Pet 2:24).

In the prophetic Psalm 22, which foretold this cry of the Lord Jesus, there is a vivid description of His death on the cross, written by inspiration centuries before. After the initial question of the psalm (v. 1), the answer is indicated in these words: "But thou art holy, O thou that inhabitest the praises of Israel" (Psalm 22:3).

God the Holy One cannot condone or tolerate sin. He must judge it, or He would compromise His own character. Therefore God chose to judge sin at the cross, visiting His wrath against sin upon His own Son rather than upon us who deserved it. At Calvary God forsook His own Son for you and me that you and I need never be forsaken.

Numerous references to the death of Christ in the Scripture show that it was penal and substitutionary. Some of these are as follows:

> I am the good shepherd: the good shepherd giveth his life for the sheep. As the Father knoweth me, even so know I the Father: and I lay down my life for the sheep (John 10:11, 15).

> But God commandeth his love toward us, in that, while we were yet sinners, Christ died for us (Rom 5:8).

> For even Christ our passover is sacrificed for us (1 Cor 5:7).

> Christ died for our sins according to the scriptures (1 Cor 15:3).

> In whom we have redemption through his blood, the forgiveness of sins, according to the riches of his grace (Eph 1:7).

> Nor yet that he should offer himself often, as the high priest entereth into the holy place every year with blood of others; for then must he often have suffered since the foundation of the world: but now once in the end of the world hath he appeared to put away sin by the sacrifice of himself (Heb 9:25-26).

This is the depth of the poverty of the Lord Jesus. The holy Son of God, who from all eternity had experienced perfect and unbroken fellowship within the Godhead as the object of the Father's perfect love, became on the cross the object of God's wrath for our sakes.

In keeping with the passages of Scripture which we have just noted, we need to pause further to meditate on the phrase "for your sakes."

"Yet for your sakes he became poor." The death of the Lord Jesus Christ on the cross, as well as all the events leading up to it, was for the world of lost men. There was no selfishness in the purpose of the Lord Jesus in coming into the world.

> God so loved the world, that he gave his only begotten Son (John 3:16).

> The Son of God . . . loved me, and gave himself for me (Gal 2:20).

The substitutionary death of the Lord Jesus is the heart of the gospel. To dismiss His death as only that of a martyr, to interpret it only as a wonderful example or moral influence for others, or to view it merely as an expression of God's hatred for sin, is to distort or deny the Holy Scriptures. Repeatedly the Word of God, as we have seen, uses terms which show beyond any doubt that the death of the Lord Jesus was a penal, substitutionary sacrifice for the sins of the world:

> And he is the propitiation for our sins: and not for ours only, but also for the sins of the whole world (1 John 2:2).

Paul tells of the compelling force of his life when he says:

> For the love of Christ constraineth us; because we thus judge, that if one died for all, then were all dead: and that he died for all, that they which live should not henceforth live unto themselves, but unto him which died for them, and rose again (2 Cor 5:14-15).

Again we are faced with the divine basis of our stewardship as Christians. May we respond in the words of Thomas O. Chisholm:

O Jesus, Lord and Saviour, I give myself to Thee,
For Thou, in Thy atonement, didst give Thyself for me;

I own no other Master, my heart shall be Thy throne;
My life I give, henceforth to live, O Christ, for Thee alone.

7

Results of His Poverty

We have been considering the statement about the grace of the Lord Jesus Christ which comes in the midst of the passage on stewardship (2 Cor 8-9). We have noted how the Scripture declares that though He was rich He became poor, and we have seen in some measure how rich He was and how poor He became.

Now we need to ask whether we are indeed rich and, if so, how rich we are.

Let us acknowledge that God has not promised earthly riches to all of His children, although He has promised to supply our needs:

> But my God shall supply all your need according to his riches in glory by Christ Jesus (Phil 4:19).

There are other riches, however, besides those which the world recognizes.

The Lord Jesus solemnly asked:

> For what shall it profit a man, if he shall gain the whole world, and lose his own soul? Or what shall a man give in exchange for his soul? (Mark 8:36-37).

An individual's salvation is of more value than all the treasures of this world. No matter how large the amount of earthly riches, they cannot satisfy the soul's hunger, nor can they last. "How much did he leave?" was the question asked about a wealthy man who had died. "Everything", was the terse reply.

> For we brought nothing into this world, and it is certain we can carry nothing out (1 Tim 6:7).

Consequently the one who has salvation through the Lord Jesus Christ is infinitely rich. These riches are immeasurable and unending. The Scripture speaks of the "riches of his grace" (Eph 1:7), of the "riches of his glory" (3:16), and of the "unsearchable riches of Christ" (3:8). These belong to the believer because he is in Christ. Paul sets forth our position in these words:

> The Spirit himself beareth witness with our spirit, that we are children of God: and if children, then heirs; heirs of God, and joint-heirs with Christ; if so be that we suffer with him, that we may be also glorified with him (Rom 8:16-17, ASV).

What are some of these heavenly riches?

Dr. Lewis Sperry Chafer in his book *Salvation* listed thirty-three possessions which are the believer's through the Lord Jesus, all of which are a part of salvation. Anyone who pages through the New Testament can discover these for himself. Salvation in all its parts is a perfect and magnificent whole; one who has even one of these possessions has all the rest, for they all form a perfect unity.

Among other things, the believer is a child of God (John 1:12), a partaker of the divine nature (2 Pet 1:4); has been translated out of the kingdom of darkness into the Kingdom of the Son of God's love (Col 1:13); has new life in Christ (Rom 6:4, 11; 2 Cor 5:17); has been forgiven all trespasses for Jesus' sake (Col 2:13); has been justified (Rom 3:24; 5:1); has received all spiritual blessings in heavenly places in Christ (Eph 1:3); is indwelt by the

Holy Spirit (Rom 8:9); has been sealed by the Spirit (Eph 4:30); has been baptized by the Spirit into the Body of Christ (1 Cor 12:13); is heir to many other marvelous possessions and positions.

Let us think about some of the elements included in these riches of salvation.

THE FORGIVENESS OF SINS

If you know the Lord Jesus Christ as your Saviour you are rich indeed in that you have experienced the forgiveness of sins.

> In whom we have redemption through his blood, the forgiveness of sins, according to the riches of his grace (Eph 1:7).

Sin separates from God. When Adam disobeyed God he was afraid and tried to hide from Him. God came calling, "Where art thou?" (Gen. 3:9). Ever since that time man by nature has been alienated from God.

No matter how much one may deny God or one's accountability to Him, the realization of guilt persists among men. Some schools of psychology seem to teach that the way to happiness is to rid oneself of guilt feelings. This can be done, it is sometimes asserted, by talking out one's feelings, trying to convince oneself and possibly others that such feelings have no basis in fact. But they do have a basis.

> For all have sinned, and come short of the glory of God (Rom 3:23).

> There is none righteous, no, not one (Rom 3:10).

> All we like sheep have gone astray; we have turned every one to his own way (Isa 53:6).

It is not sufficient to get rid of the guilt feelings. One must get rid of the guilt itself. And this no man can do.

Jesus Christ, and He alone, can do it. He has done it by being made sin for us. Because He has paid the penalty which we should have paid, we can go free. The guilt is gone. God has freely forgiven us for Jesus' sake. The sinner has now been forgiven on the basis of Christ's shed blood.

This forgiveness is a free gift of God's grace. The moment one believes on the Lord Jesus Christ, one's sins are forgiven. God says in His Word, "For I will forgive their iniquity, and I will remember their sin no more" (Jer 31:34). After experiencing God's forgiveness, King Hezekiah testified, "Thou hast cast all my sins behind thy back" (Isa 38:17). God assures us in His Word, "I have blotted out, as a thick cloud, thy transgressions, and, as a cloud, thy sins" (Isa 44:22). The psalmist rejoices, "As far as the east is from the west, so far hath he removed our transgressions from us" (Psalm 103:12).

Anyone who has received the forgiveness of sins through Jesus Christ is a partaker of the riches of heaven.

The Gift of Righteousness

Our salvation includes not only the forgiveness of sins but also the gift of righteousness. This too should make us realize how rich we are in Christ.

How righteous does one have to be to get to heaven? Men might have many answers to this question, but the only valid answer is that one has to be exactly as righteous as Jesus Christ. Nothing less will avail, and nothing more is needed.

This would drive us to despair were it not for the fact that God gives the righteousness of Christ to men as a free gift which they receive by faith.

> Him who knew no sin he made to be sin on our behalf; that we might become the righteousness of God in him (2 Cor 5:21, ASV).

> For if by one man's offence death reigned by one;
> much more they which receive abundance of grace and
> of the gift of righteousness shall reign in life by one,
> Jesus Christ. Therefore as by the offence of one judgment
> came upon all men to condemnation; even so by the
> righteousness of one the free gift came upon all men
> unto justification of life (Rom 5:17-18).

This teaching is known theologically as the doctrine of double imputation. Our sin has been imputed or reckoned to Christ. It was reckoned to Him in the sense that He died for it as if it were His own, paying the penalty which we owed and deserved to pay. At the same time, when He died He put His righteousness to our account. This imputed righteousness is ours because we are in Christ. God can therefore justify us or declare us righteous.

This is more than forgiveness. God has declared us righteous. Is this a legal fiction of some kind? Not at all. Because He has united us to His beloved Son and sees us in Him, God can righteously declare us righteous. The Scripture says concerning the gospel:

> For therein is the righteousness of God revealed from
> faith to faith: as it is written, The just shall live by faith
> (Rom 1:17).

And again:

> But now the righteousness of God without the law is
> manifested, being witnessed by the law and the
> prophets; even the righteousness of God which is by
> faith of Jesus Christ unto all and upon all them that
> believe: for there is no difference: for all have sinned,
> and come short of the glory of God; being justified freely
> by his grace through the redemption that is in Christ
> Jesus: whom God hath set forth to be a propitiation
> through faith in his blood, to declare his righteousness

for the remission of sins that are past, through the for-
bearance of God; to declare, I say, at this time his righteousness: that he might be just, and the justifier of him
which believeth in Jesus (Rom 3:21-26).

The Gift of Eternal Life

Along with the forgiveness of sins and the gift of
righteousness this wonderful salvation which we have
in Christ—which makes us so rich—includes the gift of
eternal life.

This life is referred to in many passages of Scripture.
One of the most familiar is this:

> For God so loved the world, that he gave his only
> begotten Son, that whosoever believeth in him should
> not perish, but have everlasting life (John 3:16).

Another verse which speaks of this gift of life is this:

> For the wages of sin is death; but the gift of God is
> eternal life through Jesus Christ our Lord (Rom 6:23).

Eternal life is not merely endless existence. The Bible
indicates that all men have endless existence, for there
is no such thing as the annihilation of the human soul.
The individual continues on forever, even though that
existence be in separation from God in hell.

Eternal life is that quality of life which God has and
which He gives to those who accept His Son.

> He that hath the Son hath life; and he that hath not the
> Son of God hath not life (1 John 5:12).

"And this is life eternal," said the Lord Jesus in His
high-priestly prayer to the Father, "that they might
know thee the only true God, and Jesus Christ, whom
thou hast sent" (John 17:3).

The believer does not have to wait until he dies to
receive eternal life. He has it now. The Lord Jesus said:

> Verily, verily, I say unto you, He that heareth my word, and believeth on him that sent me, hath everlasting life, and shall not come into condemnation; but is passed from death unto life (John 5:24).

In the words of Philip Doddridge:

> 'Tis done: the great transaction's done;
>   I am my Lord's, and He is mine;
> He drew me, and I followed on,
>   Charmed to confess the voice divine.

These elements—the forgiveness of sins, the gift of righteousness, and the gift of eternal life—all a part of our salvation (which includes many other elements besides), help us to realize how rich we are in the Lord Jesus Christ. Through His poverty for our sakes we have become rich in Him. Since these riches came from Him, they belong to Him, and out of these riches we are to exercise our stewardship.

8

The Christian's Willing Mind

We are considering one of the central passages of the New Testament on Christian stewardship: 2 Corinthians 8 and 9. In this passage, which tells us so much about Christian giving, we have seen the example of the Macedonian Christians and above all the example of the Lord Jesus Christ in giving Himself for us. Paul exhorted the Corinthians to follow these examples, and that is our responsibility also.

As we continue in the passage we see again that giving is not presented as a matter of compulsion:

> For if there be first a willing mind, it is accepted according to that a man hath, and not according to that he hath not (2 Cor 8:12).

Paul already knew of the initial willingness of the Corinthian Christians a year before to contribute to the particular project he was discussing, the collection for the poor saints at Jerusalem (v. 10).

Note the emphasis on personal willingness. He uses the phrases "a readiness to will" (v. 11) and "a willing mind" (v. 12). If Paul considered the tithe binding on Christians as a legal obligation, he would hardly have used such language as this. We see in the sphere of money the same approach that God uses in regard to our whole lives. He has a claim upon us, a double claim, in fact, but He prefers that we respond willingly; therefore, He will not coerce or compel.

There is also the principle of proportionate giving here, as in other parts of Scripture: "It is accepted according to that a man hath, and not according to that he hath not" (v. 12). This does not mean merely a certain set percentage for all alike, but implies that the one who has more will be able to give not only a greater amount, but also a greater proportion, than the one who has little. The amount is not the essential thing in God's sight. Variations in amount are inconsequential to Him who holds the seas in the hollow of His hand. The acceptability is in personal willingness. The one who has little of this world's goods cannot be expected to give as much as the one who is exceedingly wealthy. Experience shows that there are generous people and stingy people among both the rich and the poor. God looks on the heart. He is not arbitrary, harsh, or unreasonable in what He expects His children to do.

The man who says, "I can't give very much to the Lord, therefore I won't give anything," has not learned this principle of the willing mind. When he does learn it, he knows that God does not keep books in the same way men do. Remember that the Lord Jesus said of the poor widow that she had given more than all the others who were casting their money into the treasury (Mark 12:41-44).

"Providing for Honest Things"

The apostle Paul in his gathering of money for the work of the Lord was always careful to do things in the proper way. From what he wrote to the Corinthians it is clear that he did not administer the funds personally. They were handled by a group of men chosen by the various contributing churches, and a careful accounting was made so that no one could be suspected of using the money for personal gain:

> Avoiding this, that no man should blame us in this abundance which is administered by us: providing for honest things, not only in the sight of the Lord, but also in the sight of men (2 Cor 8:20-21).

Titus and the others mentioned in this passage had the same unselfish attitude and the same earnest care as Paul that all things should be done decently and in order.

This is another facet of stewardship. Not only is the individual believer a steward in giving, but officers of churches and other Christian organizations are stewards of God in receiving, administering, and spending funds which have been contributed to the Lord's work. A church or other Christian organization which is careless in its accounting methods, squandering funds given sacrificially by God's people, or using money for other purposes than those designated by the donors, is failing in stewardship and will be held to account by the Lord of the harvest.

In the prayer calendar of Moody Bible Institute one of the requests has been that the institute may be as right in its accounting methods as in its doctrine. This is essential in doing the Lord's work with the Lord's blessing.

Money can be a great curse or a great blessing, depending on the use made of it. Wasteful use of the Lord's money can bring reproach on the cause of Christ and can hinder the effective stewardship of children of God by causing them to withhold all giving because some stewards have been unfaithful. One of the responsibilities of the Christian steward is to give his part of the Lord's money through agencies that will exalt Christ and will use the money properly for His glory.

THE NEED FOR MUTUAL ENCOURAGEMENT

Some Christians seem to have the attitude that they resent anyone's talking to them about giving money for the Lord's work. They insist that the Holy Spirit is able to direct their giving without any assistance from others.

Of course the Holy Spirit is able to do this. Nevertheless there are clear examples in the Scriptures of Christians teaching and exhorting other Christians about the giving of money for the Lord's service. We certainly see this in Paul's statements to the Corinthians.

He reminds them of their zeal which he had experienced on a previous occasion, and encourages them to follow through, so that both they and he will not be embarrassed (2 Cor 9:1-5). There is no thought here of what we may call high-pressure methods, but there is clear authority for making the needs known to Christians and for instructing them in their responsibility of stewardship.

One who does this is not depriving believers of anything, certainly not defrauding them. Rather, he is helping them to come to a place of greater blessing. We have seen that giving is referred to as a "grace" (2 Cor 8:7). This is always something extremely good. But how many Christians fall short in this respect, not having learned the truth of the statement of the Lord Jesus, "It is more blessed to give than to receive" (Acts 20:35).

We all need reminders of these things from time to time. Even though we know the general principles of stewardship and are aware of our responsibility, in this area—as in so many others in Christian living—we tend to forget or to grow lax. "The world is too much with us." We are greatly concerned with the financial struggle for daily living, and we forget the promise of our gracious heavenly Father to care for us and supply our needs.

So we ought not to take it amiss when those commissioned by God remind us of our stewardship responsibilities. They have a solemn obligation from the Lord to do so, and they must remember in doing so that they too are stewards. If they can point us to the Word of God and show us the blessings God has for those who do His will, they can give a good account of their stewardship.

SPARINGLY OR BOUNTIFULLY?

What many of us do not seem to realize is that the only thing we can really keep is what we give away to God. We hug our possessions to ourselves, thereby thinking we are gaining something, but time soon shows what fools we were.

Christian stewardship is compared in the text to sowing and reaping a crop:

> But this I say, He which soweth sparingly shall reap also sparingly; and he which soweth bountifully shall reap also bountifully (2 Cor 9:6).

We all know in the natural realm that if we sow very little seed we should not expect an abundant harvest. A farmer who scatters only a small amount of seed sparingly in only a few places in his field need not be surprised if he goes hungry.

God is trying to show us that the very same principle applies in Christian stewardship. The one who withholds from God cannot expect a great reward. The Macedonian Christians, as we have seen, were exceedingly liberal in their giving, even though by earthly standards most of them were poor people. God saw to it that they did not lose out.

Stewardship is a part of faith. Can we trust God for

today and tomorrow as well as for eternity? Paul, in writing to the Philippians, thanking them for the gift they had sent him, tells them that he is thankful not only for what he has received, but also for that which accrues to them through their giving:

> But I rejoiced in the Lord greatly, that now at the last your care of me hath flourished again. . . . Not because I desire a gift: but I desire fruit that may abound to your account (Phil 4:10, 17).

This is the context for a verse which is often quoted:

> But my God shall supply all your need according to his riches in glory by Christ Jesus (Phil 4:19).

God is perfectly able to supply all our needs under all circumstances. The point here, however, is that we need not fear because of our own personal needs to give to the Lord's work when He asks us to do so, because God will provide for those if we put Him first and obey the promptings of the Holy Spirit.

The question is one of values, earthly as against heavenly. Do we have enough faith to see that which is invisible, to realize that only what we give to God is ours for all eternity?

"According as He Purposeth in His Heart"

Is it possible to do the work of the Lord unhappily? Obviously it is, from the number of discontented Christians that we meet. In this text we are told another principle of Christian stewardship:

> Every man according as he purposeth in his heart, so let him give; not grudgingly, or of necessity: for God loveth a cheerful giver (2 Cor 9:7).

Paul does not say, "Every man must pay a tithe." He does not say, "Every man is to give what he is obligated to give." No, the decision is left up to the individual believer. Some would think that God is placing His work on very precarious ground in doing this. Not at all. He is not dependent on men; He has chosen to bless them by permitting them to have a part in His work of their own free will.

Therefore we have no right to tell other Christians what they ought to give. We can instruct others in the Word of God and its principles of Christian stewardship, but we cannot make the decision for another concerning the amount of the gift to God. It is "every man according as he purposeth in his heart."

But this is not a natural heart. It is a redeemed heart, a heart which has been renewed by the Spirit of God. David said:

> Delight thyself also in the LORD; and he shall give thee the desires of thine heart (Psalm 37:4).

God will not merely give a man what he desires but will also shape the very desires themselves. A man who is yielded to God will desire, without compulsion or coercion, to do what God wants him to do. This paradox is inexplicable, but completely believable—because God makes it plain in His Word—that the man most completely subject to the will of God is the freest of all men.

The principle is the same as that enunciated in these words:

> Work out your own salvation with fear and trembling. For it is God which worketh in you both to will and to do of his good pleasure (Phil 2:12-13).

Hence there need be no fear that such a man will not please the Lord. He can be safely trusted to make his own decision. There is no law, God reminds us, against anything which is the fruit of the Holy Spirit (Gal 5:22-23).

"Not Grudgingly, or of Necessity"

The principle has been established from this text that Christian giving is to be a matter of individual decision. This purpose to give, we note now, is to be marked by joyful willingness. If a man is cajoled or coerced into giving what he does not really want to give, he does not experience the personal blessing which God wants him to have.

"Not grudgingly," the text tells us. Christian stewardship is not a matter of "have to" or even of "ought to." It is a matter of "want to." We have no right to say to others, "You must give"; but, rather, we can say, "You have the great privilege of giving to the Lord if you will." Christian workers have no right, and certainly no mandate from God, to browbeat others into giving to the Lord's work.

"Not grudgingly" describes the personal attitude of the giver, the subjective side. "Or of necessity" describes the objective side; no compulsion is laid upon the individual. Anyone who tries to put other believers under the law in this respect is going contrary to the plain statement of the Word of God.

What a difference it makes in the Christian's life when this blessed truth becomes a part of his experience! That liberty which is the gift of the Holy Spirit is then realized in this aspect of living. Stewardship becomes a joyous privilege, not an irksome duty.

One of the tragic examples in Scripture of those who gave grudgingly is seen in the record of Ananias and Sapphira, who wanted to have a reputation for giving all while they withheld part from God. Peter said:

> Whiles it remained, was it not thine own? And after it
> was sold, was it not in thine own power? Why hast thou
> conceived this thing in thine heart? Thou hast not lied
> unto men, but unto God (Acts 5:4).

A wonderful example of ungrudging giving is seen in
the time of David:

> Then the people rejoiced, for that they offered will-
> ingly, because with perfect heart they offered willingly
> to the LORD (1 Chron 29:9).

David's prayer at this time is also instructive:

> For all things come of thee, and of thine own have we
> given thee (1 Chron 29:14).

"A CHEERFUL GIVER"

We have seen in our text the words "For God loveth a
cheerful giver." This declaration raises a question. Does
not God love everyone? Yes, we know that God loves all
men; the proof of this is in His giving His Son to die for
the sins of the world.

> For God so loved the world, that he gave his only
> begotten Son, that whosoever believeth in him should
> not perish, but have everlasting life (John 3:16).

> But God commendeth his love toward us, in that,
> while we were yet sinners, Christ died for us (Rom 5:8).

> And he is the propitiation for our sins: and not for ours
> only, but also for the sins of the whole world (1 John 2:2).

> Herein is love, not that we loved God, but that he loved
> us, and sent his Son to be the propitiation for our sins (1
> John 4:10).

Scripture teaches, however, that God has a special
love for those who know and belong to the Lord Jesus,
who said:

> He that hath my commandments, and keepeth them,
> he it is that loveth me: and he that loveth me shall be
> loved of my Father, and I will love him, and will man-
> ifest myself to him. If a man love me, he will keep my
> words: and my Father will love him, and we will come
> unto him, and make our abode with him (John 14:21, 23).

God has a special love toward the cheerful giver. Such a giver puts God first and recognizes that His cause takes precedence over every other claim, even the most legitimate. This is the overflow of a heart filled with gratitude to God, who has done so much for us.

Shakespeare's King Lear exclaims:

> How sharper than a serpent's tooth it is
> To have a thankless child.

Sad to say, God has many thankless children. But the one who has been taught by the Holy Spirit the enormity of his lost condition, the horror of the pit from which he has been rescued, and the magnitude and perfection of salvation through Christ, responds joyfully. This is the joy of the Lord in action, that reaches the pocketbook and causes that which—under other conditions—would be so jealously guarded for self-satisfaction to be poured forth freely for the honor of Christ, as Mary of Bethany poured out the precious "ointment of spikenard" on His feet (John 12:3; cf. Matt 26:7; Mark 14:3).

The cheerful giver, the one who gives without compunction or inner restraint, but with liberality and satisfaction, is in this respect like God Himself, who did not withhold His greatest treasure, but willingly offered up His beloved Son for lost mankind.

> He that spared not his own Son, but delivered him up
> for us all, how shall he not with him also freely give us
> all things? (Rom 8:32).

This is the kind of giving already mentioned by the apostle, as manifested by the Macedonian believers:

> How that in a great trial of affliction the abundance of their joy and their deep poverty abounded unto the riches of their liberality. Praying us with much intreaty that we would receive the gift (2 Cor 8:2, 4).

"ALL SUFFICIENCY IN ALL THINGS"

The peculiar thing about so many of us is that we forget that no man can outgive God. We realize, of course, that God will guide the yielded Christian to pay his debts fully and promptly and not to shirk any legitimate obligation toward any man. To refuse to pay just debts on the ground that the money is to be given to the service of Christ is to dishonor the Lord.

This, however, is another aspect. We are thinking of the Christian who says he would like to give to the Lord's work but who hesitates because he is afraid he will not have enough for himself. Too often we "mind earthly things" (Phil 3:19); too often we forget that our citizenship is in heaven (Phil 3:20); too often the "cares of this world, and the deceitfulness of riches, and the lusts of other things" (Mark 4:19) choke the Word and keep it from having its full effect in our lives.

If I obey joyfully the call of the Spirit of God concerning my Christian stewardship, can I doubt that my heavenly Father will provide for me? In the passage we have been considering there is a word of instruction and encouragement for us about this:

> And God is able to make all grace abound toward you; that ye, always having all sufficiency in all things, may abound to every good work (2 Cor 9:8).

"God is able," Paul assures us, "to make all grace abound toward you." This is an eternal principle. God will be no man's debtor. The one who gives to God will receive back in full measure and much more besides. "Prove me now," God challenged Israel (Mal 3:10). "Will I have enough for myself?" asks the fainthearted Christian. "That ye, always having all sufficiency in all things, may abound to every good work," answers our God.

Can one afford to give to God? The Lord Jesus said:

> Give, and it shall be given unto you; good measure, pressed down, and shaken together, and running over, shall men give into your bosom. For with the same measure that ye mete withal it shall be measured to you again (Luke 6:38).

Again He promised:

> Verily I say unto you, There is no man that hath left house, or parents, or brethren, or wife, or children, for the kingdom of God's sake, who shall not receive manifold more in this present time, and in the world to come life everlasting (Luke 18:29-30).

The true motive in giving is not to receive something in return; it is love toward God. Giving merely in order to get is not really giving; it is just a means of getting (and with such a motive one is unlikely even to get). Nevertheless one cannot give to God without getting something in return. That is the nature of God.

GREATER GLORY TO GOD

The section of 2 Corinthians 9:9-14 shows us how our giving results in God's glory. The willing, cheerful giving of God's people to His cause brings greater glory to Him through the thanksgiving of many who are helped. Who can calculate the effect of a dollar given prayerfully to buy tracts through which some learn of Christ and accept Him? Or money given for the support of a

pioneer missionary in some far-off land, who brings the
Word of life to those who sit in darkness? Or funds
designated for the training of some of God's choice
young servants, that they may be equipped and prepared to take the Gospel of Christ to the ends of the
earth?

If God will not forget, but will honor, the cup of cold
water given "only in the name of a disciple" (Matt
10:42), we can be assured that nothing truly given to
God will ever be wasted. Like a great revolving fund, our
part, given with gratitude and prayer, although in itself
it may be small, will keep on working for the Lord. The
effect even of a tract upon a life may cause that life to be
fruitful in reaching other lives, who in turn may reach
out to others. The consequences go on and on for His
glory, and in heaven many will have cause to rejoice and
to thank God even for the little that we gave.

Yes, God will multiply our seed sown (2 Cor 9:10).
The God who could feed the 5,000 with five loaves and
two fish can also perform miracles with our pittance.
"Little is much when God is in it" has often been truly
said.

Our failing is that we, like Israel of old, limit the Holy
One (see Psalm 78:41). It is recorded of our Lord Jesus in
Nazareth that He "did not many mighty works there
because of their unbelief" (Matt 13:58). We need an
effervescent faith, welling up from deep within through
the power of the Holy Spirit, that will respond in a
divinely wrought abandonment.

This is not recklessness. No license is given in the
Scripture for neglect of one's family or failure to dis-
charge ordinary human obligations. On the contrary,
God severely condemns the believer who does not provide for his own household (1 Tim 5:8). But what we are

thinking of is rather a counting of the cost which moves one paradoxically not to count the cost for Christ's sake.

"HIS UNSPEAKABLE GIFT"

This great section on Christian stewardship (2 Cor 8-9) is brought to a close and a climax by the exclamation of the apostle: "Thanks be unto God for his unspeakable gift" (2 Cor 9:15).

We are brought back again to the true wellspring of Christian giving. "We love him," the Scripture tells us, "because he first loved us" (1 John 4:19). In the same way, we give because He first gave.

God so loved . . . that he gave (John 3:16).

The gift of God is eternal life through Jesus Christ our Lord (Rom 6:23).

If a man is not thankful for God's gift, he will not be a giver, no matter how much he may be urged and importuned by men. Even if he were to give to the Lord's work under pressure, it still would not be truly a gift to God such as God wants. God's gift to us is the source and motivation of our giving to Him.

The gift of God is indescribable. The word *unspeakable* in our text refers to that which cannot be put into words. Language is inadequate to describe all the Lord Jesus is in His person and His work. Isaiah tells us that His "name shall be called Wonderful" (Isa 9:6).

He is wonderful in His Person. There is no one else like the Lord Jesus Christ. He is the unique One, the Son of God and Son of man, the God-man, God manifest in the flesh (see John 1:1, 14; 1 Tim 3:16). Having all the attributes of deity, He also shares all the sinless characteristics of humanity. He is the Holy One, the loving One, the merciful One, the compassionate One. He

"went about doing good, and healing all that were op-
pressed of the devil" (Acts 10:38).

He is wonderful in His work. No one else could do
what the Lord Jesus did. The psalmist said of all mankind, "None of them can by any means redeem his
brother, nor give to God a ransom for him" (Psalm 49:7).
But the Lord Jesus Christ could and did redeem. He gave
"his life a ransom for many" (Matt 20:28; Mark 10:45).
He is the Man Christ Jesus, "who gave himself a ransom
for all" (1 Tim 2:6). "When he had by himself purged our
sins, [he] sat down on the right hand of the Majesty on
high" (Heb 1:3).

What more can we say except to join the apostle in
exclaiming, "Thanks be to God for his unspeakable
gift."

9

Money–for Self or for God?

We have given considerable attention to 2 Corinthians 8 and 9 as the central passage in the Scripture on the Christian stewardship of money. One must not get the impression, however, that this is the only passage on the subject. While this little book is not presuming to claim exhaustive coverage, we shall now look briefly at some other scripture portions which supplement what we have already discovered in the Word.

SYSTEMATIC GIVING

In 1 Corinthians Paul introduced the topic of the collection for the saints on which he dwelt at greater length in 2 Corinthians.

> Now concerning the collection for the saints, as I have given order to the churches of Galatia, even so do ye. Upon the first day of the week let every one of you lay by him in store, as God hath prospered him, that there be no gatherings when I come (1 Cor 16:1-2).

This instruction of Paul brings to our notice the principle of regularity in giving to the Lord. The setting, of course, is that of Paul's third missionary journey with the great project which occupied a large part of his attention, the offering for the poor saints in Jerusalem. This was to be a love and thank offering to the Jewish believers from the Gentile Christians in recognition of all the spiritual benefits they had received from Jewish Christians and missionaries of the gospel. In Romans, written during the same period, Paul explained:

> But now I go unto Jerusalem to minister unto the saints. For it hath pleased them of Macedonia and Achaia to make a certain contribution for the poor saints which are at Jerusalem. It hath pleased them verily; and their debtors they are. For if the Gentiles have been made partakers of their spiritual things, their duty is also to minister unto them in carnal things (Rom 15:25-27).

Paul shows that the regular setting aside of money for the Lord's work is preferable to sporadic or infrequent drives for money. Each believer, in careful recognition of God's bounty to him, is to set aside regularly what he believes God would have him give to Himself.

The first day of the week is specifically mentioned because this is the resurrection day, the special day of the new creation—the Lord's Day—just as the Sabbath, the seventh day, was the special day of commemoration of the old creation. On this day believers meet together in memory of the Lord Jesus, to worship Him and to meditate on His Word. Is it not fitting then that the believer should make this also a vital part of his worship and service?

"As God hath prospered him." This statement calls attention again to the fact that all things come from God.

> Every good gift and every perfect gift is from above, and cometh down from the Father of lights, with whom is no variableness, neither shadow of turning (James 1:17).

But Isn't Money Evil?

Objections may be raised by some against so much

discussion of money in the Christian life. After all, it may be asked, does not the Scripture say that money is evil? How then can money be used to glorify God?

Several times, it is true, there is reference in the New Testament (at least in the King James Version) to "filthy lucre." A bishop in the church must be a man who is "not greedy of filthy lucre" (1 Tim 3:3). Deacons also must be men "not greedy of filthy lucre" (1 Tim 3:8). The same thing is said of bishops or elders in Titus 1:7—"not given to filthy lucre." In that same passage false teachers are said to teach "things which they ought not, for filthy lucre's sake" (Titus 1:11). Peter's exhortation to elders is in this same vein:

> Feed the flock of God which is among you, taking the oversight thereof, not by constraint, but willingly; not for filthy lucre, but of a ready mind; neither as being lords over God's heritage, but being ensamples to the flock (1 Pet 5:2-3).

When we look at these passages in the original language we see that the word used in 1 Timothy 3:3 means literally "not loving money" or "not avaricious." This word is found only twice in the New Testament, the other occurrence being in Hebrews 13:5, where the King James Version translates it as "without covetousness." In both of these places the New American Standard Bible translates "free from the love of money."

A different word is used in 1 Timothy 3:8, which the New American Standard Bible translates literally as not "fond of sordid gain." The same adjective form is used in Titus 1:7, and the noun and adjective from the same root in Titus 1:11, for which the New American Standard Bible again uses the literal translation "sordid gain." The very same root is used adverbially in 1 Peter

5:2 and is translated by the New American Standard as in the other passages.

One can readily see from these passages that the motive of the person involved and his use of the money are the things which make it "filthy" or "sordid." The officer of the church who performs his service only for personal gain thereby causes the money which he receives to become "filthy" in God's reckoning.

There is nothing either good or bad, moral or immoral, about money as such. The moral quality is given to it by men's attitudes toward it and the uses they make of it.

The Lord Jesus solemnly warned, "Ye cannot serve God and mammon" (Matt 6:24; Luke 16:13). *Mammon* is an Aramaic word referring to money or riches. The explanation of this is seen in the word "serve" and in the context:

> No one can serve two masters; for either he will hate the one and love the other, or he will hold to one and despise the other. You cannot serve God and mammon (Matt 6:24, NASB).

The Lord Jesus in these words is showing two utterly contrasting principles for living. Is the believer to be a servant of God or a servant of money? Money ought to be a servant or a tool; man ought not to be a slave to it. Too many men, however, have become enslaved to their own covetousness and have consequently failed to serve God. "Ye cannot serve God and mammon."

"THE LOVE OF MONEY"

God does not say that money is evil. What He says is that "the love of money" is a root of every kind of evil (1 Tim 6:10). The sin of covetousness is sometimes linked in the Scripture with gross sins of immorality, as being equally heinous in God's estimation (see Mark 7:21-23; 1 Cor 6:9-10). Paul speaks of "covetousness, which is idolatry" (Col 3:5), and reminds us that some disciples of the Lord have so coveted money that "they have erred from the faith, and pierced themselves through with many sorrows" (1 Tim 6:10).

More than once in the Scripture we are warned that the pursuit of riches can lead men astray. One example is this:

> They that will be rich fall into temptation and a snare, and into many foolish and hurtful lusts, which drown men in destruction and perdition (1 Tim 6:9).

This does not mean that poor men as such are better than rich men, or that riches in themselves are sinful; it does mean that wealth brings a new kind of temptation into the life of a man which may cause him to forget his obligations to God.

Riches cannot be trusted. They cannot bring lasting satisfaction. Solomon paints a graphic picture of the rich man who lacks the health to enjoy his riches:

> There is an evil which I have seen under the sun, and it is common among men; a man to whom God hath given riches, wealth, and honour, so that he wanteth nothing for his soul of all that he desireth, yet God giveth him not power to eat thereof, but a stranger eateth it: this is vanity, and it is an evil disease (Eccles 6:1-2).

The Christian is charged not to "trust in uncertain riches, but in the living God, who giveth us richly all things to enjoy" (1 Tim 6:17). He can make use of the money which God has given him. As a steward of God's bounty he can spend it in the right way, not heaping up treasures here on earth, but following these instructions:

> That they do good, that they be rich in good works,
> ready to distribute, willing to communicate; laying up
> in store for themselves a good foundation against the
> time to come, that they may lay hold on eternal life (1
> Tim 6:18-19).

It is the principle we have seen so often—only what
we give to God will be ours throughout all eternity.

MAKING FRIENDS BY THE MAMMON OF UNRIGHTEOUSNESS

No discussion of stewardship would be complete
without some notice of the parable of the unjust steward
as given by the Lord Jesus in Luke 16:

> Now He was also saying to the disciples, "There was a
> certain rich man who had a steward, and this steward
> was reported to him as squandering his possessions.
> And he called him and said to him, 'What is this I hear
> about you? Give an account of your stewardship, for you
> can no longer be steward.'
>
> "And the steward said to himself, 'What shall I do,
> since my master is taking the stewardship away from
> me? I am not strong enough to dig; I am ashamed to beg. I
> know what I shall do, so that when I am removed from
> the stewardship, they will receive me into their homes.'
>
> "And he summoned each of his master's debtors, and
> he began saying to the first, 'How much do you owe my
> master?' And he said, 'A hundred measures of oil.' And
> he said to him, 'Take your bill, and sit down quickly and
> write fifty.' Then he said to another, 'And how much do
> you owe?' And he said, 'A hundred measures of wheat.'
> He said to him, 'Take your bill, and write eighty.'
>
> "And his master praised the unrighteous steward be-
> cause he had acted shrewdly; for the sons of this age are
> more shrewd in relation to their own kind than the sons
> of light.

"And I say to you, make friends for yourselves by means of the mammon of unrighteousness; that when it fails, they may receive you into the eternal dwellings. He who is faithful in a very little thing is faithful also in much; and he who is unrighteous in a very little thing is unrighteous also in much. If therefore you have not been faithful in the use of unrighteous Mammon, who will entrust the true riches to you? And if you have not been faithful in the use of that which is another's, who will give you that which is your own?

"No servant can serve two masters; for either he will hate the one, and love the other, or else he will hold to one, and despise the other. You cannot serve God and mammon" (Luke 16:1-13, NASB).

Our Lord does not commend the steward in this parable for his injustice; it was his human master—*that lord*—who commended him, because he evidently admired what we might call his unmitigated gall. The Lord Jesus comments, "The children of this world are in their generation wiser than the children of light" (Luke 16:8).

What the steward did was technically legal because he had been entrusted with the control of his master's property. He discounted the debts which were owed to his master, thus not only liquidating those frozen assets, but at the same time making friends of those whose debts he had reduced.

The Lord Jesus, pointing out how the steward had used *unrighteously* for his own advantage the funds entrusted to him, shows us how we, as His stewards, can use *righteously* for our own advantage the funds entrusted to us:

And I say unto you, Make to yourselves friends of the mammon of unrighteousness; that, when ye fail, they

may receive you into everlasting habitations (Luke
16:9).

This mammon which we have is a part of the unrighteous world system in which we live, even though we as
Christians are not a part of it. Mammon can be used
righteously for the glory of God and the good of others.
How wonderful to meet someone someday in heaven
who will greet you with thankfulness because the
money you gave was the instrument God used in getting
the gospel to him! This is making friends by means of
the mammon of unrighteousness.

This is the context in which the Lord Jesus further
shows that money is to be a servant, not a master. A man
who allows money to control him cannot serve God, for
"no servant can serve two masters" (Luke 16:13).

The principle is also spelled out here that a man's
faithfulness in the use of money is a test of his dedica-
tion and his usefulness in other spheres:

> He that is faithful in that which is least is faithful also
> in much: and he that is unjust in the least is unjust also in
> much. If therefore ye have not been faithful in the un-
> righteous mammon, who will commit to your trust the
> true riches? (Luke 16:10-11).

LAYING UP TREASURES

In His Sermon on the Mount the Lord Jesus Christ laid
down the principle of laying up treasures.

There are only two places to lay up treasures. One is
on earth. This is the only place known to the natural
man. These treasures, while they may seem to be wonderful, ultimately fail, either because they melt away or
because the possessor has to go away and leave them.
Hence the Lord Jesus warns:

> Lay not up for yourselves treasures upon earth, where

moth and rust doth corrupt, and where thieves break through and steal (Matt 6:19).

The Lord is not prohibiting necessary and careful saving for taking care of one's needs and the needs of one's dependents. Prudent management of finances is a virtue. Nevertheless, the outcome even of the godly man's amassed wealth, if it is merely amassed and not put into the service of God, is that it will pass away.

James depicts the future misery of ungodly men who amass wealth through oppressing others:

Go to now, ye rich men, weep and howl for your miseries that shall come upon you. Your riches are corrupted, and your garments are motheaten. Your gold and silver is cankered; and the rust of them shall be a witness against you, and shall eat your flesh as it were fire (James 5:1-3).

Here is a vivid picture of wealth unused for good purposes. The corrosion of unused wealth, which could have been used in the service of God and man, stands as an accusing witness against its owners.

Any man who makes earthly wealth his only goal will fail to find lasting happiness. Like all earthly desires, this one is self-multiplying and consequently self-defeating. No matter how much there may be, there is always the desire for more. How many have made shipwreck of their lives through pursuing this one ambition!

There is another place to lay up treasures for oneself, a place not known at all to the unbeliever, and a place all too dim for many a Christian. Paul tells us that we are to look "not at the things which are seen, but at the things which are not seen: for the things which are seen are temporal; but the things which are not seen are eternal" (2 Cor 4:18).

"Not Rich Toward God"

One of the parables of the Lord Jesus shows the ironic plight of the man who heaps up treasures on earth. It concerns the rich man whose crops were so abundant that he lacked storage space. To accommodate all the surplus he planned to tear down his barns and build larger ones. He supposed that then all would be well. The parable is found in Luke 12:16-34. The man's soliloquy is very instructive:

> And I will say to my soul, Soul, thou hast much goods laid up for many years; take thine ease, eat, drink, and be merry (Luke 12:19).

There is no indication that this man was an exceptionally wicked man. Probably he was not. He was no doubt industrious and had worked hard to amass his earthly possessions. But he had overlooked the most important thing. He was prepared for earth's tomorrow but had not given any thought at all to any tomorrow elsewhere.

> But God said unto him, Thou fool, this night thy soul shall be required of thee: then whose shall these things be, which thou hast provided? (Luke 12:20).

The point of the parable is expressed by the Lord Jesus in these words:

> So is he that layeth up treasure for himself, and is not rich toward God (Luke 12:21).

The earthly riches, the object of so much concern and effort, can become utterly meaningless in an instant of time. How much more important it is to be "rich toward God"!

After telling the parable the Lord Jesus went on to show that the believer should not have anxiety about the necessities of earthly life. The King James Version, which uses the expression "take no thought" (Luke 12:22), is not clear enough here. The wording of the original means "have no anxiety." The Lord Jesus does not condemn careful planning but forbids worrying. God is able to provide the food, clothing, and shelter which we need. Our attention should be riveted primarily on that which is lasting.

We who know the Lord Jesus Christ should have insight which will make us different from unbelievers around us:

> For all these things do the nations of the world seek after: and your Father knoweth that ye have need of these things. But rather seek ye the kingdom of God; and all these things shall be added unto you (Luke 12:30-31).

"TREASURES IN HEAVEN"

As we have seen, the Lord Jesus commands us not to lay up for ourselves treasures on earth. We are not to be like the rich fool, who was well prepared for the future on earth but found that he had no earthly future.

The only place where treasure can be laid up and really guaranteed against loss is in heaven in the presence of God. The Lord Jesus said:

> But lay up for yourselves treasures in heaven, where neither moth nor rust doth corrupt, and where thieves do not break through nor steal: for where your treasure is, there will your heart be also (Matt 6:20-21).

This is not a matter of salvation. The Christian already has been saved by the grace of God on the basis of Christ's shed blood. The question now is: How is he going to live his life for the Lord Jesus? Where is his heart?

Paul exhorts the Colossians to "seek those things which are above, where Christ sitteth on the right hand of God" (Col 3:1). The believer has a heavenly salvation, a heavenly calling, a heavenly destiny, a heavenly citizenship. How strange then and how ironic to find him wrapped up completely in the things of earth!

Paul continues, "Set your affection on things above, not on things on the earth" (Col 3:2).

The believer's standing is perfect. He is complete in the Lord Jesus Christ; identified with Christ, not only in His death, but also in His glorious resurrection. His state or condition ought to measure up to his exalted standing. There are numerous exhortations to this end in Scripture, including these:

> Only let your conversation [manner of life] be as it becometh the gospel of Christ (Phil 1:27).

> I therefore . . . beseech you that ye walk worthy of the vocation wherewith ye are called (Eph 4:1).

The stewardship of money, as we have said before, helps to test the reality and depth of our Christian experience. We may say that we have our minds fixed on heavenly things, but we can hardly expect others to believe us if our actions prove that our greatest concern is to get ahead in the world. We are brought face to face with reality by the reminder of the Lord Jesus, "Where your treasure is, there will your heart be also."

10

Stewardship of Body and Mind

Earlier in our study we noted Scripture which shows that the believer is exhorted to present his body to God (Rom 12:1-2). Numerous passages in the Word of God teach us that we are to recognize our stewardship in the possession and use of both body and mind.

THE BODY A STEWARDSHIP

In contrast to many human philosophies, some of which deprecate the body and some of which overexalt it, the Bible emphasizes the value and the sanctity of the human body and the importance of using it for God. That the body is a stewardship is proved by such passages as this:

> For we must all appear before the judgment seat of Christ; that every one may receive the things done in his body, according to that he hath done, whether it be good or bad (2 Cor 5:10).

Like the Old Testament priest who had the blood of the sacrifice applied to the tip of his right ear, the thumb of his right hand, and the big toe of his right foot (Lev 8:23-24), the believer has been set apart to the service of God. He says in effect:

> My ears have been redeemed by the blood of Christ to hear the Word of the Lord.

91

My hands have been redeemed by the blood of
Christ to do the work of the Lord.

My feet have been redeemed by the blood of
Christ to walk in the way of the Lord.

No one can do anything apart from his body; hence
the body is often used as an instrument of sin. This is the
teaching of Paul in Romans 6, where he exhorts that the
members of the body which have been used formerly as
instruments of unrighteousness should now be used as
instruments of righteousness for God.

In a similar passage in 1 Corinthians 6 he shows how
the body is used by unsaved people (and, tragically,
sometimes by believers) for immoral purposes. He
warns:

> Now the body is not for fornication, but for the Lord;
> and the Lord for the body. And God hath both raised up
> the Lord, and will also raise up us by his own power.
> Know ye not that your bodies are the members of Christ?
> Shall I then take the members of Christ, and make them
> the members of an harlot? God forbid. What? Know ye
> not that he which is joined to an harlot is one body? For
> two, saith he, shall be one flesh. But he that is joined
> unto the Lord is one spirit. Flee fornication. Every sin
> that a man doeth is without [outside] the body; but he
> that committeth fornication sinneth against his own
> body (1 Cor 6:13-18).

In his warning against the misuse of the body for
immoral purposes, Paul shows the evil effects of sexual
immorality on the body itself and proceeds to set forth
the real condition of the body of the believer:

> What? Know ye not that your body is the temple of the
> Holy Ghost which is in you, which ye have of God, and
> ye are not your own? For ye are bought with a price:
> therefore glorify God in your body, and in your spirit,
> which are God's (1 Cor 6:19-20).

A temple is a dwelling place of God. In the Old Testament economy, the nation of Israel, at the command of God, had a temple which was the visible meeting place of God and His people. There the sacrifices were offered, and toward that place prayer was made (see 1 Kings 8:27-30). God dealt with His people through ceremonies and signs.

In the New Testament the Church *is* a temple, not a building of wood and stone, but a sanctuary of living stones.

> Know ye not that ye are the temple of God, and that the Spirit of God dwelleth in you? (1 Cor 3:16).

> To whom coming, as unto a living stone, disallowed indeed of men, but chosen of God, and precious, ye also, as lively stones, are built up a spiritual house, an holy priesthood, to offer up spiritual sacrifices, acceptable to God by Jesus Christ (1 Pet 2:4-5).

> Now therefore ye are no more strangers and foreigners, but fellowcitizens with the saints, and of the household of God; and are built upon the foundation of the apostles and prophets, Jesus Christ himself being the chief corner stone; in whom all the building fitly framed together groweth unto an holy temple in the Lord: in whom ye also are builded together for an habitation of God through the Spirit (Eph 2:19-22).

The text which we have considered from 1 Corinthians 6 shows that not only is the whole Church a temple of God but the body of each believer is such a temple. God dwells in every Christian in the Person of the Holy Spirit.

Since God is holy, His dwelling place should be holy. No defilement should enter. If I weigh each action in the light of this truth—that I am living in the presence of God, and that His Holy Spirit is in some way involved in every use I make of my body—this should move me to live a godly life.

> For this is the will of God, even your sanctification, that ye should abstain from fornication: that every one of you should know how to possess his vessel in sanctification and honour; not in the lust of concupiscence, even as the Gentiles which know not God: that no man go beyond and defraud his brother in any matter: because that the Lord is the avenger of all such, as we also have forewarned you and testified. For God hath not called us unto uncleanness, but unto holiness (1 Thess 4:3-7).

THE MIND A STEWARDSHIP

The unsaved person is subject not only to the desires of the flesh, but also of the mind (Eph 2:3). This is not to say that the Christian is immune to either of these lines of temptation, but he has a new nature and the empowerment of the Holy Spirit to overcome temptation.

Sometimes, even when we can recognize the heinousness of unclean fleshly desires, we are not aware of the sinfulness of some of the desires of the mind. It is the tendency of the human heart to be lifted up with pride and to scorn any restraint from God.

Scripture contains many warnings against pride.

> Every one that is proud in heart is an abomination to the LORD (Prov 16:5).

> Pride goeth before destruction, and an haughty spirit before a fall (Prov 16:18).

> But he giveth more grace. Wherefore he saith, God resisteth the proud, but giveth grace unto the humble (James 4:6, quoted from Prov 3:34).

> Yea, all of you be subject one to another, and be clothed with humility: for God resisteth the proud, and giveth grace to the humble (1 Pet 5:5).

This pride and willfulness will reach their climax in the future when Antichrist is manifested briefly. He is described as one "who opposeth and exalteth himself above all that is called God, or that is worshipped" (2 Thess 2:4).

The Lord Jesus revealed what the capacity of the human mind is for evil when He said:

> But those things which proceed out of the mouth come forth from the heart; and they defile the man (Matt 15:18).

The believer has received a renewed mind from God. His thought patterns have been changed so that he has a new attitude toward God, toward his environment, and toward himself.

Yet there is a constant temptation to "mind earthly things" (Phil 3:19). We are exhorted to set our minds "on things above, not on things on the earth" (Col 3:2). The mind which is fixed on Jesus Christ is freed from shackles that would hinder it from reaching its highest capacity. The Apostle Paul's aspiration was to bring his mind into complete subjection to the Lord Jesus Christ:

> Casting down imaginations, and every high thing that exalteth itself against the knowledge of God, and bringing into captivity every thought to the obedience of Christ (2 Cor 10:5).

We are to use our renewed minds, yielded to the indwelling Holy Spirit, for the glory of our Saviour. The mind is indeed a stewardship. If we allow our minds to dwell on those things which are unclean and unworthy, we shall bring dishonor to the Lord Jesus and shame to ourselves. The only way to avoid the wrong use of the mind is to persist in the right use of it, for the mind is never a blank tablet. Paul exhorts:

> Finally, brethren, whatsoever things are true, what-
> soever things are honest, whatsoever things are just,
> whatsoever things are pure, whatsoever things are
> lovely, whatsoever things are of good report; if there be
> any virtue, and if there be any praise, think on these
> things (Phil 4:8).

"Be ye transformed," the Scripture commands, "by
the renewing of your mind" (Rom 12:2).

The Stewardship of Talents

In His Olivet discourse, delivered to the disciples as
representatives of the nation of Israel shortly before His
death, the Lord Jesus gave a parable which is usually
referred to as the parable of the talents. The word *talent*
in this connection means a sum of money. To one servant were given five talents, to another two, and to
another one (Matt 25:14-30).

In modern English usage the word *talent* has come to
mean a gift or one's natural ability. It is apparent that
this passage in the Bible influenced this usage.

The principle set forth in the parable applies in any
dispensation or any circumstances. Consequently we
can apply it, without wresting the Scripture, to the fact
that all our abilities are a stewardship from God. Other
passages plainly declare the same truth. These are
examples:

> For who maketh thee to differ from another? And what
> hast thou that thou didst not receive? Now is thou didst
> receive it, why dost thou glory, as if thou hadst not
> received it? (1 Cor 4:7).

> But thou shalt remember the Lord thy God: for it is he
> that giveth thee power to get wealth (Deut 8:18).

Paul's testimony can be that of every Christian:

> But by the grace of God I am what I am (1 Cor 15:10).

What is the teaching of the parable of the talents? It is that what God gives to us is to be used for His glory. The man who had five talents made five additional talents; the man who had two talents gained two additional talents. They improved the opportunities which they had. We can apply this, as we have said, to the stewardship of our abilities as well as to the stewardship of money.

Undoubtedly many Christians are working at less than their capacity; they have not begun to develop their potential for God. When we think of financiers and captains of industry who literally wear themselves out by ceaseless efforts to amass an earthly fortune and to gain earthly prestige, when we see the arduous labors that men will undertake in order to be elected to office in the governments of this world, how pallid our efforts for Christ sometimes appear!

The hymn writer asked, "Must I be carried to the skies on flowery beds of ease?" Some of us answer an unqualified and shameless "yes" when we ought to respond with a forthright and resolute "no."

His Commendation of Faithfulness

What is it that the Lord especially commends in the case of the two servants with the five talents and the two talents respectively? The answer is obvious; it is their faithfulness.

> Well done, thou good and faithful servant: thou hast been faithful over a few things, I will make thee ruler over many things: enter thou into the joy of thy lord (Matt 25:21).

Note that the master said the same thing to the two-talent man that he said to the five-talent man. The amount involved was not the essential. Faithfulness was the essential. "It is required in stewards, that a man be found faithful" (1 Cor 4:2).

Faithfulness pertains to the here and the now. Some of us sometimes think that if we had more money we would be better stewards for the Lord; of if we were in some other place or had some other capabilities, we would serve Him better.

Apart from some direct and marvelous intervention of God this never eventuates. The man who is unfaithful with a hundred dollars will most likely also be unfaithful with a million. The man who does not serve the Lord in his own country will not be likely to serve Him across the ocean. Faithfulness is tested in the little things. The Lord Jesus said:

> He that is faithful in that which is least is faithful also in much: and he that is unjust in the least is unjust also in much (Luke 16:10).

Faithfulness is not an abstract ideal; it is a patient, careful, continuous attention to every detail. Are we able to be trusted with the larger things of God? Perhaps the reason the Lord has not given us greater funds to administer and larger opportunities for service is that He knows He cannot trust us with those things.

Our responsibility then is to be faithful with what we have now. We are not to be like the one-talent man, who blamed the master for his own failure. God's justice may seem strange to some, but it is justice nevertheless:

> For unto every one that hath shall be given, and he shall have abundance: but from him that hath not shall be taken away even that which he hath (Matt 25:29).

Jim Elliot, one of the martyrs among the Aucas, said, "He is no fool who gives what he cannot keep to gain what he cannot lose."

11

Stewardship of Time, Speech, and Action

The stewardship of life clearly implies stewardship of every aspect and facet of life. One would have to make the detailed application in his own experience. The yielded Christian will constantly find new dimensions to this total question. As he discovers new areas of living which he has not yet consciously surrendered to the Lord Jesus Christ, he will strive to make that explicit which was already implicit in his presentation of his body to God.

This chapter seeks to explore briefly several more implications.

ACCOUNTABILITY FOR TIME

Although most of us would be at a loss to know how to define time, we are confronted often in the Scripture with its reality and the necessity of using it properly. The eternal God is the Author of time and it is to Him we are responsible for what we do with it. David said to God, "My times are in thy hand" (Psalm 31:15).

In considering his accountability to God for time, man is to reckon on the present. The past cannot be undone (although past sins can be forgiven through Jesus Christ), and we cannot control the future, but we can act in the present. In reference to the gospel, God says:

> Behold, now is the accepted time; behold, now is the
> day of salvation (2 Cor 6:2).

Men are prone to put things off, particularly decisions
about spiritual matters. The Roman governor Felix
procrastinated in this way. He said to Paul, "Go thy way
for this time; when I have a convenient season, I will call
for thee" (Acts 24:25). That time never came; so far as we
know, Felix never did accept the Lord Jesus.

God instructs His children that they are to make the
most of time. "The time is short," Paul admonishes the
Corinthians (1 Cor 7:29). We are urged to redeem the
time "because the days are evil" (Eph 5:16). This means
that we are to buy up every opportunity to serve the Lord
Jesus Christ.

There are many different uses of time, and there must
be in the life of every Christian times of recreation,
relaxation, and rest, even some times of doing nothing.
But such periods are to be for a purpose. There is no
place for wasting time or "killing" time if we are to give
the best account of our stewardship. It is in this area we
often err by spending too much time on things which
may be good in themselves but which hinder us from
doing the better or the best.

While we can instruct one another from the Word of
God, we cannot command other Christians about the
specific use of their time and we should avoid unscriptural judging. How the Christian uses his time is between him and his Lord. God may not direct another
man to use his time in the same way as He directs me.

Many years ago some Christians probably criticized
Alexander Cruden for spending so much time in listing
all the occurrences of so many different words in the
Scripture. No doubt some said he ought to be out
preaching and witnessing and winning souls to Christ

instead of what he was doing. Think, however, of the marvelous help *Cruden's Concordance* has been to multitudes of Christians in getting to know the Bible and in becoming prepared for all kinds of Christian service.

> For as the body is one, and hath many members, and all the members of that one body, being many, are one body: so also is Christ. And the eye cannot say unto the hand, I have no need of thee: nor again the head to the feet, I have no need of you (1 Cor 12:12, 21).

Moses prayed, "So teach us to number our days, that we may apply our hearts unto wisdom" (Psalm 90:12). Each day for the believer is a time of opportunity, a time of challenge. Paul reminds us of our responsibility when he says:

> And that, knowing the time, that now it is high time to awake out of sleep: for now is our salvation nearer than when we believed. The night is far spent, the day is at hand: let us therefore cast off the works of darkness, and let us put on the armour of light (Rom 13:11-12).

There is no going back for the Christian, but he can go forward joyfully and triumphantly as he puts his total dependence on the Lord Jesus Christ.

> The path of the just is as the shining light, that shineth more and more unto the perfect day (Prov 4:18).

ACCOUNTABILITY FOR SPEECH

We are told in Scripture that we are accountable to God for our words. The Lord Jesus Christ, before He ascended to heaven, commissioned His disciples to be His witnesses. He said:

> But ye shall receive power, after that the Holy Ghost is come upon you: and ye shall be witnesses unto me both

in Jerusalem, and in all Judea, and in Samaria, and unto
the uttermost part of the earth (Acts 1:8).

This witnessing is incumbent upon every child of
God. Not all have the same field of service; not all have
the same breadth of opportunity; but all are to be witnesses. We have the responsibility of being faithful in
the place where God has put us.

The Lord Jesus showed the gravity of this when He
said:

> Whosoever therefore shall confess me before men,
> him will I confess also before my Father which is in
> heaven. But whosoever shall deny me before men, him
> will I also deny before my Father which is in heaven
> (Matt 10:32-33).

The early Christians went everywhere preaching the
Word. In their daily occupations, no matter what the
conditions and circumstances, they made Christ
known. A mere word, of course, not backed up by godly
Christian living, may be of little force; but if we do not
let our light shine before men, how can they glorify our
Father who is in heaven, since they cannot see Him and
do not know Him? (see Matt 5:16).

Our speech, then, is indeed a sacred stewardship. We
have been entrusted with the gospel, not only for ourselves, but also for the eternal benefit of others. Paul's
questions are searching:

> How then shall they call on him in whom they have
> not believed? And how shall they believe in him of
> whom they have not heard? And how shall they hear
> without a preacher? And how shall they preach, except
> they be sent? As it is written, How beautiful are the feet
> of them that preach the gospel of peace, and bring glad
> tidings of good things! (Rom 10:14-15).

He goes on to show that only as the child of God gives

out the Word of God can men come to saving faith in Christ: "So then faith cometh by hearing, and hearing by the word of God" (Rom 10:17).

May we be like the disciples of old, who, when they were commanded to be silent, boldly replied, "For we cannot but speak the things which we have seen and heard" (Acts 4:20).

Sound Speech

Not only are we stewards of speech to say the right thing for the Lord, but also to refrain from saying the wrong thing. Often in the Scripture we are warned against rash words. The Lord Jesus indicated we are to be judged for the things we say:

> But I say unto you, That every idle word that men shall speak, they shall give account thereof in the day of judgment. For by thy words thou shalt be justified, and by thy words thou shalt be condemned (Matt 12:36-37).

The believer is exhorted to use "sound speech, that cannot be condemned" (Titus 2:8). James has much to tell us about the use of the tongue. Its propensities to evil are boundless; it sins by inciting others to sin, directly by such sins as lying and blasphemy, and by applauding the sins of others.

> And the tongue is a fire, a world of iniquity: so is the tongue among our members, that it defileth the whole body, and setteth on fire the course of nature; and it is set on fire of hell (James 3:6).

Many would suppose it unnecessary for the Holy Spirit to command Christians to stop lying and other sins of speech, but it is sadly true that He must command this:

> Wherefore putting away lying, speak every man truth with his neighbour (Eph 4:25).

> Lie not one to another, seeing that ye have put off the old man with his deeds (Col 3:9).

The Scripture repeatedly warns us against evil speaking. The following is an example of such a warning:

> Let no corrupt communication proceed out of your mouth, but that which is good to the use of edifying, that it may minister grace unto the hearers (Eph 4:29).

As we become increasingly aware of our stewardship in this vital area, we can pray from the heart as the psalmist prayed: "Set a watch, O LORD, before my mouth; keep the door of my lips" (Psalm 141:3).

When we yield our speech to Him we become an occasion of praise to our Lord instead of a stumbling block to others, and that which we say will exemplify this beautiful description: "A word fitly spoken is like apples of gold in pictures of silver" (Prov 25:11).

DOING THE WILL OF GOD

As we have discovered many times in our study, the subject of Christian stewardship is far broader than the giving of money, although that is an integral part of it. Stewardship takes in the whole of life. It involves doing the will of God in thought, word, and deed.

Surely every Christian wants in some measure to do the will of God. Many are perplexed, however, about God's will. The average Christian young person is often troubled about God's will for his life. Some older Christians are not as concerned about this as they should be. How can I know what the will of God is for me when there are so many possible roads to take, so many different decisions to be made day after day after day? In spite of my perplexity and uncertainty I do want to do His will.

This is a part of our stewardship because we are not

our own. Our lives have been entrusted to us to use for Him to whom we really belong.

> For the love of Christ constraineth us; because we thus judge, that if one died for all, then were all dead: and that he died for all, that they which live should not hence-forth live unto themselves, but unto him which died for them, and rose again (2 Cor 5:14-15).

But how can we know the will of God for us? We cannot expect that He will speak to us miraculously with an audible voice or give us some unusual sign, because He has already spoken and has given us His Word in written form. The Bible, the written Word of God, is where we discover the will of God. A principle that permeates the Bible concerning the discovery of His will is that God makes His will known to those who obey Him.

Do I really want to know the will of God for me? Then I must obey that which I already know to be His will. In these meditations we have learned many things from the Bible about God's will for our stewardship. We have the responsibility to obey what God has told us. The Lord Jesus said to His disciples concerning His teachings, "If ye know these things, happy are ye if ye do them" (John 13:17). God's Word also tells us:

> Therefore to him that knoweth to do good, and doeth it not, to him it is sin (James 4:17).

We see the obedience of faith in the life of Abraham:

> By faith Abraham, when he was called to go out into a place which he should after receive for an inheritance, obeyed; and he went out, not knowing whither he went (Heb 11:8).

Abraham did not know where he was going, but he

knew the God who had called him to go, and he knew
that He knew.

> I'd rather walk in the dark with God
> Than walk alone in the light;
> I'd rather walk by faith with Him
> Than walk alone by sight.

"The Will of God in Christ Jesus"

Do I really want the will of God for my life? Am I really
convinced that my life is a stewardship? Then I must be
obedient to that which I know to be His will.

One suggestion for each of us is to search the Scriptures with the definite intention of finding those statements which declare the will of God and then to proceed
to act upon them. The Lord Jesus said:

> If any man will do his will, he shall know of the
> doctrine, whether it be of God, or whether I speak of
> myself (John 7:17).

We cannot withhold consent as we encounter God's
will. We cannot come to Him with the response that if
He will show His will we shall then decide whether we
will do it or not. Obedience is prerequisite to discovery.

There are many passages of Scripture which tell some
definite element or elements in the will of God for us.
One such passage is the following:

> Rejoice evermore. Pray without ceasing. In every
> thing give thanks: for this is the will of God in Christ
> Jesus concerning you (1 Thess 5:16-18).

"Rejoice evermore." The joy of the Lord is quite different from the happiness of the world, which depends on
circumstances. This joy is a gift from God. Because He is
unchanging and unchangeable, joy can be constant,
even when mingled with affliction and heaviness of

heart. This is a paradox of which the world knows nothing.

Joy can be manifested in the exercise of our stewardship. The Macedonian Christians, as we have seen, were exceedingly joyful in their liberality. In view of the fact that God makes this joy possible, I can respond in the enablement He gives me. This is certainly the will of God for me. But if I face life glumly, how can I expect my heavenly Father to reveal further aspects of His will, since I am not obeying that which I already know to be His will? "This is Thy will, Lord, but I don't like it and I'm not going to do it; show me something else that's Thy will which I may like better!" I should not be surprised to be left in darkness, since I have rejected the light that He gave.

"Pray without ceasing." This speaks of an attitude. Our whole life as Christians should be one of dependence on our heavenly Father who knows what our needs are before we ask. Nevertheless He wants us to ask:

> Be anxious for nothing, but in everything by prayer and supplication with thanksgiving let your requests be made known to God. And the peace of God, which surpasses all comprehension, shall guard your hearts and your minds in Christ Jesus (Phil 4:6-7, NASB).

The way of the world is the way of fretting and worrying; it is the way of scheming and "pulling strings." Worry, because it turns one inward, is self-inflating because it somehow deceives the worrier into thinking that by his worry he can influence the course of events. "Look at me—I'm so worried!" One wise old Christian said, "I'm getting along all right since I quit trying to help Almighty God run the universe."

The Christian way is the way of trust and obedience.

These qualities look toward God; they acknowledge that there is no strength or wisdom in self, but that one is completely dependent on Him.

> Wherefore seeing we also are compassed about with so great a cloud of witnesses, let us lay aside every weight, and the sin which doth so easily beset us, and let us run with patience the race that is set before us, looking unto Jesus the author and finisher of our faith; who for the joy that was set before him endured the cross, despising the shame, and is set down at the right hand of the throne of God (Heb 12:1-2).

This too has a direct bearing on our stewardship. When we commit our requests to our heavenly Father, He will give us His peace and He will provide. The text tells us that His peace "passeth all understanding" or "surpasses all comprehension." In the natural realm there are many things which have to be experienced in order to be known. How could one describe color to someone who was born blind, or music to someone born deaf? One cannot describe the "peace of God" to someone who has never experienced it through faith in Jesus Christ. It cannot be explained or even understood, but it can be known.

> Thou wilt keep him in perfect peace, whose mind is stayed on thee: because he trusteth in thee (Isa 26:3).

> Peace I leave with you, my peace I give unto you: not as the world giveth, give I unto you. Let not your heart be troubled, neither let it be afraid (John 14:27).

> The fruit of the Spirit is . . . peace (Gal 5:22).

"Oh, but I'd rather go my own way, Lord; show me something else!" This is no way to find the will of God.

"In everything give thanks: for this is the will of God in Christ Jesus concerning you." The unhappy, complaining Christian is obviously not doing all the will of God that he knows. Like the murmuring Israelites in the wilderness he will miss out on much of God's blessing.

> They soon forgat his works; they waited not for his counsel: but lusted exceedingly in the wilderness, and tempted God in the desert. And he gave them their request; but sent leanness into their soul. Many times did he deliver them; but they provoked him with their counsel, and were brought low for their iniquity. Nevertheless he regarded their affliction, when he heard their cry: and he remembered for them his covenant, and repented according to the multitude of his mercies (Psalm 106:13-15, 43-45).

The Christian life is a life of thanksgiving, or ought to be. The will of God is the best thing for any of us. Since He has made His will known in these and many other particulars, it is essential for us to obey.

Epilogue

If we ever had the idea that stewardship had to do only with money, we surely have found enough from God's Word to show what a limited view this was. Although our study has been relatively brief and far from exhaustive, we have seen enough to realize that there is no detail of life outside the circle of stewardship. This subject is all-comprehensive.

In a sense I am a steward whether I want to be or not, since it is a fact that I have nothing of my own. Everything has been received from God. But God wants me to be a conscious, willing steward—to receive everything from His hand thankfully, to acknowledge my complete dependence, and to return everything joyfully back to Him to His everlasting praise and glory.

Not my own! That is the essence of stewardship. To be

conscious at all times that all I am and have is a sacred trust from God through the Lord Jesus Christ my Saviour and to rejoice unreservedly in that consciousness!

Someday we all shall stand before the Lord Jesus Christ to give an account of our stewardship. The efforts, and even the trials, of this present time will seem insignificant then in comparison with His approval.

> Therefore judge nothing before the time, until the Lord come, who both will bring to light the hidden things of darkness, and will make manifest the counsels of the hearts: and then shall every man have praise of God (1 Cor 4:5).

> For we must all appear before the judgment seat of Christ; that every one may receive the things done in his body, according to that he hath done, whether it be good or bad (2 Cor 5:10).

> For none of us liveth to himself, and no man dieth to himself. For whether we live, we live unto the Lord; and whether we die, we die unto the Lord: whether we live therefore, or die, we are the Lord's. For to this end Christ both died, and rose, and revived, that he might be Lord both of the dead and living. But why dost thou judge thy brother? Or why dost thou set at nought thy brother? For we shall all stand before the judgment seat of Christ. For it is written, As I live, saith the Lord, every knee shall bow to me, and every tongue shall confess to God. So then every one of us shall give account of himself to God (Rom 14:7-12).

May we be like the Apostle Paul, the great steward of the grace of God, who said:

> I press toward the mark for the prize of the high calling of God in Christ Jesus (Phil 3:14).